"Audacious and mind-stretching, Crossman sees our reliance on the printed word coming rapidly to an honorable end. He offers valuable reassurances about our humanistic prospects after the book has faded in use. He invites us to imagine co-existence with very 'smart' equipment in an oral culture that sounds very rewarding. His original scenario warrants open-minded consideration by all who appreciate the thoroughness of the extraordinary on-going changes we must turn to advantage." –*Arthur B. Shostak, Professor of Sociology and Director, Center for Employment Futures, Drexel University, Philadelphia, Pennsylvania*

"William Crossman's *VIVO [Voice-In/Voice-Out]* is a welcome addition to the discussion about voice-recognition technology and the social implications of talking computers." –*Edward Cornish, President, World Future Society, Bethesda, Maryland*

"If you are an educator, you need to read this book. Every day we see students fail at skills we value and succeed at skills we dismiss. What William Crossman sees, however, is an evolutionary step forward, the shift from alphabetic culture to an electronic-oral future that will offer many liberations. Of course educators are notorious cynics and hand-wringers, except for the genuinely visionary ones; William Crossman may be one of those. Whether, ultimately, he's right or not, the future he envisions will challenge your cynicism and might even shake your despair." –*Les Gottesman, Director of General Education, Golden Gate University, San Francisco, California*

"Futures thinking is about presenting creative and courageous ideas challenging our basic thought-patterns which are considered as self-evident. William Crossman's book about the rising oral culture with the help of talking computers is doing exactly that!" –*Dr. Mika Mannermaa, President, Futures Studies Mannermaa Ltd., Docent in Futures Research, Turku School of Economics, Finland*

"Talking computers replace written language? 'Not on my watch,' I cry to my shelves of books. But I was raised in a different technological age. So, like it or not, I need to account for my students' attitudes towards reading and writing and to understand how they may gain access to the information, ideas and resources they will need far into the 21st Century. While William Crossman's ideas aren't ones I want to hear, they are provocative in ways that force us to consider a future which will not look like the past we have come from. This book should generate discussions critical to our students' futures." *–Jean Miller, Professor of English, De Anza Community College, Cupertino, California*

"While preparing a paper for a conference on the idea that writing (but not to the same extent reading) is about to become largely obsolete, I came across your paper in *The Futurist*, and now your institute. I am thrilled to see that you have explored these possibilities in great detail, and I will of course study and quote your work. My first question at this juncture is: Is your book out yet, or when will it be?" *– Professor Dan Sperber, Directeur de Recherche, CNRS, Institut Jean Nicod (CNRS et EHESS), Paris, France; author, Explaining Culture*

"Futurist Jim Dator says that 'Any useful idea about the future should appear to be ridiculous.' Your concept of a totally verbal society and the death of the written word scandalized the writer in our group who verbalized how ridiculous it sounded. However, the more one reads, the stronger your case becomes. It has huge implications for the structure of society. Now it is the illiterate, the dyslexic and the blind who suffer from our emphasis on reading and writing. In 2050 it may be those who can not verbalize well who will be in the risk group!" *–Natalie Dian, Futurist, Visionscentret Framtidsbygget AB, Göteborg, Sweden*

VIVO
[Voice-In/Voice-Out]

VIVO
[Voice-In/Voice-Out]

The Coming Age
of Talking Computers

William Crossman

Regent Press
Oakland, CA

To contact William Crossman and/or the CompSpeak 2050 Institute for the Study of Talking Computers and Oral Cultures, go to website <**www.compspeak2050.org**>.

First Printing 2004

Publisher's Cataloging-in-Publication

Crossman, William.
    VIVO (voice-in/voice-out) : the coming age of talking computers / William Crossman.
    p. cm.
    Includes bibliographical references and index.
    LCCN 2004093358
    ISBN 1-58790-100-5

    1. Information society--Forecasting. 2. Speech processing systems--Social aspects. I. Title.

HM851.C76 2004   303.48'33
                   QBI04-200238

Cover design by Roslyn Abraham and William Crossman, with assistance from Barbara Barnett and Rudy Lemcke. Credit also to the photographers whose photos adorn the cover.
Typesetting and graphics by Roslyn Abraham, D.G. Park, and Lauren Agresti.

Articles by William Crossman based on ideas in this book have appeared in numerous publications, including: *Frontiers of the 21ˢᵗ Century, Teaching and Learning in a Network World, World Forests and Technology, The Futurist, Community College Week, Good Weekend magazine—Sydney (AU) Morning Herald, Futura, The Next Twenty Years Futures, and Our World: The New Millennium.* For a complete list, access the author's website.

Disclaimer: This book, its author William Crossman, and the CompSpeak 2050 Institute are not connected with and/or do not endorse any specific product, business, corporation, agency, institution, offline or online entity, website, or individual that is named or uses the words "Vivo," "voice-in/voice-out," "talking computer," "Vivolutionary," "compspeak," or any other concept or word that appears in this book—except such as are created by, and/or are copyrighted by, and/or are held as intellectual property rights by, and/or are approved contractually in writing by William Crossman.

Manufactured in the U.S.A.
REGENT PRESS · 6020-A Adeline Street · Oakland, CA 94608 · www.regentpress.net

To my dear mother, Estelle

Special thanks to Lea Weinstein for her insightful comments on the manuscript. Thanks also to the following colleagues and friends whose constructive critiques, input, and efforts helped this book to reach completion: Roslyn Abraham, Barbara Barnett, Peter Bishop, Camo Bortman, Tony Cerazzo, Chinosole, Edward Cornish, Allan Crossman, Natalie Dian, Mickey Ellinger, Tom Frey, Chukk Garard, Les Gottesman, "Cassie Gray," Ray Grott, Adele Hurvitz, Dan Johnson, Michael Larsen, Harry Lefever, Rudy Lemcke, Mika Mannermaa, Ann M. Marie, Clifton Marsh, Jean Miller, Michael Novick, D. G. Park, Art Shostak, John Smart, Dan Sperber, John Trimble, Mark Weiman, and Abigail Woodward. And thanks to the many students, conference participants, and others who discussed this book's ideas with me over the years.

Table of Contents

Introduction

Caution, readers! Enter and explore *VIVO [Voice-In/Voice-Out]*'s wild terrain of ideas at your own risk. As one who has crossed and recrossed this book's landscape and has survived to tell about it, let me offer up a brief perspective and a couple of tips for a successful journey.

Several books published since 1990 have tried to predict how computers will affect literacy. Some see the proliferation of people using the Internet and writing e-mail, together with the growing number of school computer writing labs and online book sales, as proof that literacy will thrive. Others see computers' irresistible interactive visual displays and sound as submerging text and prompting literacy's decline, which they view as a tragic loss.

VIVO [Voice-In/Voice-Out] is the first book to take a *positive* look at how talking computers, VIVOs, will make text/written language obsolete, replace all writing and reading with speech and graphics, democratize information flow worldwide, and recreate an oral culture by 2050.

As readers, you will tour that oral culture and observe how

VIVOs will change the ways we'll do almost everything—and even who we'll be, our human consciousness. Along the way, you'll get a taste of the new oral-aural-visual processing skills we'll need to survive in the fast-approaching post-script world.

Central to the book's reaching these objectives is its identification and analysis of the four "engines" that are working together to replace written language/text with VIVOs in the electronically-developed countries. Like four horses pulling a coach, these "engines" are continuously pulling, pushing, and supporting each other and, by doing so, are propelling an unstoppable historical trend.

The "engines":

(1) Evolutionarily, our biology and psychology forever direct us to seek speech-based methods for storing, retrieving, and communicating information.

(2) Technologically, we are driven to develop technologies that enable us to access information by speaking and listening. In addition, we tend to replace older technologies with newer ones that will do the same job more quickly, efficiently, and universally. Written language/text is *a technology*—an ancient technology whose basic job is to store and retrieve information. Once we understand and accept this idea, we will probably be more open to the idea that written language, like all technologies, can be replaced.

In fact, since the late 1800s, we have been rapidly introducing replacements for written language in the form of radio, phonograph/stereo, film, video, telephone, computers, and other non-text technologies that allow us to use speaking, listening and looking at graphics to access information. In the 21st Century, VIVOs will complete the replacement process.

(3) Young people in the electronically-developed countries

are irreversibly rejecting text as their technology of choice for accessing information, and are replacing it with speech-based and non-text visual technologies. They've abandoned letter writing in favor of the telephone, and books in favor of TV, movies, CDs, and computer graphics and games. Now that spoken e-mail is available, they will likewise abandon written e-mail. In order to process information using these non-text technologies, young people are developing, albeit unsystematically, the very VIVOlutionary skills they'll need in order to function in the oral culture that they're creating.

(4) Eighty percent of adults worldwide are functionally nonliterate. In the 21st Century, these billions of people will require text-free computer technology that will allow them to store and retrieve information—a huge, potential market that will continue to drive VIVO research and development.

Part I of this book focuses on developing a portrait of these four "engines." But instead of describing each "engine" separately, one after the other, Part I spirals through them, first touching briefly on all of them in Chapter 1, then revisiting, deepening, and integrating them in Chapters 2 – 4.

Unlike Part I, Part II focuses on specific human activities and how VIVOs will change the ways we'll perform them over the coming decades. Part II's chapters forecast the new approaches to information access, the arts, literacy's global political-economic role, even mathematics. Chapter 5 presents the eight VIVOlutionary skills we'll need to access information using VIVOs; it also discusses how, as we develop these skills, we'll change our human consciousness. Although Part I provides the foundation for the forecasts in Part II, readers can skip to Part II and enjoy any chapters there that interest them without having read all of Part I.

When I present these ideas to audiences of readers-writers, they usually respond with anxious questions and comments, including the following. If most people won't be able to read and write by mid-21st Century, won't the power elite then be able to reserve written language for themselves and use it to keep information from the general population? And won't this create a society where a small number of people wield power and control over everybody else?

My answer is that *this is the situation that we have today*, and it is the situation that we have had since the creation of written language 10,000 years ago. The great majority of the world's population is still being deprived of literacy skills because those in power continue to view literacy as a privilege rather than a right. In the 21st Century, however, the power elites themselves will choose speech and VIVOs over text and text-driven computers to access information and to attempt to control its flow.

On the positive side, I see VIVOs opening up specific potential opportunities for the Have-Nots of the world: opportunities for accessing information that was formerly accessible only to the print-literate, opportunities for instantaneous translation of speech from one language to another, and opportunities for people with disabilities to access information without having to read and write it. It all depends, of course, on whether the Have-Nots will be able to gain access to talking computers.

I, like many people I know, dream of—and, through our actions, try to bring about—a world where freedom, equality, justice, and peace reign. It is not this dream that I'm questioning throughout this book; I'm questioning whether written language is the best technology for accessing the information that we'll need to make this dream come true.

Using written language, I am able to communicate with only

20 percent of the world's people—the 20 percent that is functionally literate—which is not nearly enough people to realize this dream. Using a VIVO, I will be able to communicate with everyone, nonliterate or literate, with disabilities or without, who has access to a VIVO. Though it will take more than mere communicating to achieve freedom, equality, justice, and peace, being able to break through the text barrier and communicate with greater numbers of people isn't a bad place to start.

In Chapter 1 of this book, I say that I admire and respect everyone who is struggling to acquire literacy skills, and I urge everyone to go to school, stay in school, and learn to read and write. For the next decade or so, the ability to write and read will still be necessary to access information that will be available mainly in the form of text. After that, literacy skills will become less and less important as talking computers supersede the written word.

When I started developing this book's main ideas in 1992, the voice-recognition technology wave was barely visible on the horizon, and everyone I spoke to about *VIVO [Voice-In/Voice-Out]*'s thesis treated it as science fiction. Perhaps, to some degree, I did too. Now that the wave is starting to break over our heads, its force, and the places to which it will carry us, are becoming clearer and more real, less fictitious but equally fantastic.

I've chosen a less formal style for *VIVO [Voice-In/Voice-Out]*—one closer to ordinary speech than to academic writing. I hope readers will appreciate the chance to retrieve the stored information here with your minds' ears as well as your eyes—a good exercise in VIVOlutionary learning.

I invite readers to communicate with me and others about this book's ideas. Tell your VIVOs to access the website for my CompSpeak 2050 Institute for the Study of Talking Computers and Oral Cultures. Speak your minds, and journey well!

No Words on Their Cereal Box: A Day in the Life of a 21st Century Oral-Culture Family

I t's a cool Thursday morning in March, 2050. The family's voice-in/voice-out—VIVO—computers begin to serenade Kathy and her children, Mary Beth and Thomas, with wake-up music. Their VIVOs, like all talking computers in 2050, lack keyboards because information exchange is text-free. Data and commands are inputted by voice; outputted data is heard and seen, but not read.

This morning, however, the serenading VIVOs don't appear to be heard by Kathy and the children. No one is budging. Getting up at 7:00 a.m. in the year 2050 isn't any easier than it was in 2005. After five minutes, with everyone still in bed, the VIVOs change their music menu to something louder and livelier. Five more minutes go by without anyone stirring.

Now the computers get serious, junking their musical approach for some strong verbal encouragement. Kathy hates hearing this particular spoken message because it mimics the words and tone that her own parents used to use to wake her when she was a child—which is exactly why Kathy programmed their VIVOs with that message. Ten seconds of the VIVOs' parental scolding is enough to pry everyone out of bed.

Kathy starts to ask her VIVO what time it is but has a coughing fit instead, so she glances over at the visual time display on her VIVO's screen. Lacking written numerals, it shows the 07:10 time as |...|. |˙ |...| , utilizing four glowing LORNS (location relative numeral substitutes). No written numerals? Not to worry. It's 2050!

Kathy, Mary Beth, and Thomas shower, dress, and, head to the kitchen for breakfast. Thomas reaches for the cereal box and fills his bowl. The box is covered with eye-catching holographics, but no writing, no words. None of the other food packaging on the table has writing on it either. Along with its graphics, each package sports a brand-identification symbol and, in place of the old 20th Century bar code, Kathy's DNA code, which allows the food suppliers to electronically fill, price, bill, and deliver the goods that Kathy ordered online using her VIVO. Neither Thomas nor Mary Beth has ever read a cereal box.

The absence of written language isn't limited to the time display on Kathy's bedside VIVO and the food packaging in the kitchen. This family's apartment is no different from most other families' apartments in mid-21st Century electronically-developed countries: written language doesn't appear anywhere. Like almost all of their neighbors, co-workers, and schoolmates, Kathy, Mary Beth, and Thomas can't read or write.

Neither twelve-year-old Mary Beth, who is finishing her last year of college, nor Thomas, age 4, who is completing fifth grade, has ever learned to write or read. Kathy's schools didn't teach writing or reading either, but thinking that it would be fun to learn, she joined an extra-curricular Written Language Club for a year when she was ten and became quite expert at writing and reading.

Now, though, she has forgotten almost all the written language that she learned because she hasn't practiced or used it in over twenty-five years. Kathy keeps telling her friends that if her children ever decided to take up reading and writing as a hobby, then maybe she'd join them and get back into it again. Uh-huh, Kathy, we'll believe it when we see it.

When breakfast is over, Kathy moves to her favorite chair and asks her satellite-driven VIVO to recite her new messages and display their accompanying graphics on her wall screen. Kathy finds it hard to believe that, only forty-five years ago, people were still writing and reading e-mail and letter carriers were still placing letters in people's home mailboxes.

After she listens to her messages, Kathy will spend the rest of the morning at home working at her job: mentally composing her daily online spoken "op-ed column" and then reciting it into her VIVO. She's amused that her daily "journalistic" recitations are still referred to in the old 20th Century print terms, but her bosses at the Daily Post Access believe that promoting her spoken pieces as "op-ed columns" adds a quaint touch that attracts a larger audience. The irony is that very few of the people who regularly access Kathy's views on the Daily Post Access even know what the words "op-ed" or "column" (not to mention "Post" or "journalistic") mean or refer to.

Mary Beth checks her new messages on her wrist VIVO and on the tiny flipdown graphics monitor lodged in her cap's visor, then waves goodbye, rushes out the door, jumps on her bicycle, and heads off to soccer practice. Her backpack is stuffed with her shin guards and cleats, her lunch, and her hand drum. After lunch, she and her friends will spend the afternoon at the community's Nature Preserve Park helping to care for the plants and animals, improvising music together, and just hanging out. Mary Beth prefers to wait until after dinner to log onto her college classes, using her online VIVO wall monitor at home to see and talk with her professors and college classmates.

Thomas wants to go swimming at the community pool in the afternoon, so he decides to do his schoolwork this morning. Logging onto the VIVO wall unit near his bed, he joins a Comparative Cosmology class that's comparing a 5000-year-old Nubian theory of the universe, Albert Einstein's 145-year-old Theory of Relativity, and Benita Lopez's most recent revision (2048) of the Unified Field Theory. After a few seconds online, Thomas is debating the pros and cons of the various theories with his teacher and schoolmates, and storing on his VIVO the parts of the discussion that he'll want to re-access.

After Kathy's "column" and Thomas' schoolwork are finished, they get into their electromagnetic hovercar and head to Kathy's mother's apartment for lunch and a visit. As they pull away from the curb, Kathy speaks her password to the car's VIVO computer, placing the car's motion functions under the control of the regional AUTOLINK system. Kathy tells the VIVO that their destination is her mother's apartment; then, she and Thomas lean back and relax. VIVO and AUTOLINK take over from there.

Along the roads and expressways that Kathy's car is traveling, there are no written signs designating street names, expressway exits, or speed limits. They're not necessary since the car's movement is being electronically controlled and its location constantly monitored by satellites. If Kathy wants to know the name of the street they are on, she will just ask her VIVO. As a visual backup, their VIVO monitor displays their trip both as an icon moving along a (wordless) roadmap and as an actual satellite view of their car moving along the highway.

At times, Kathy asks her VIVO to comment on traffic and weather conditions, street names and numbers, speed limits, and points of interest along the route. At other times, she glances at the car's speed, RPMs, and energy level depicted as bar graphs—no written numerals here either—located on her car's dashboard. Of course, Kathy always keeps the VIVO's spoken-graphic interrupt function turned on to alert her of any immediate or impending mechanical failures, traffic problems, or weather emergencies.

And no billboard words in sight! True, there are plenty of roadside billboards, though they aren't really boards, and no bills are posted on them. They are, in fact, giant VIVO display screens teeming with moving visual ads and corporate logos. If Kathy and Thomas wish, they can access the billboards' spoken messages through their car's VIVO, but right now Kathy prefers her VIVO to be quiet while she chats with Thomas about his schoolwork and their visit with Grandma Marie.

As they pull up in front of her mother's house, Kathy—as usual—reminds Thomas not to speak too quickly when he talks to Grandma Marie. What Kathy considers speed-speaking is becoming Thomas' ordinary speaking style, and Kathy isn't too happy about it. Thomas assures Kathy that he'll try to, in his words, "keep my voice-out" slow enough for Grandma to understand. They ring the doorbell, walk in, and find Grandma Marie sitting at the kitchen table reading a novel and sipping coffee.

Grandma Marie learned to read as a child in school in the 1980s and got hooked on it. After college, she taught Spanish to high schoolers for twenty-five years but took early retirement when her school district—deciding that VIVOs had made foreign-language study unnecessary—dropped her courses from the curriculum. Afterward, Grandma Marie free-lanced as an aloud-reader, transferring difficult-to-scan pre-21st Century manuscripts onto VIVO networks. But she eventually lost that job, too, to advancing technology when even the most difficult hand-written materials were able to be electronically scanned onto VIVO networks, and the last generation of aloud-readers was laid off.

Reading, along with long-distance running, has continued as Grandma Marie's favorite pastime, but she has been having a harder and harder time finding books to read. Every couple of months, she orders more books through her online Antiques Shopping Network, but she can barely afford her beloved books anymore as they've become rarer and their prices have escalated.

Grandma Marie fills three bowls with hot soup and, as always, asks Thomas how his classes are coming along. As Thomas, taking care to speak slowly, describes his classes, Grandma Marie looks at Kathy and exclaims, "Einstein? In the fifth grade? For four-year-olds?" As they eat, Grandma Marie recalls how home schooling and distance-learning by computer were just starting to become popular in the 1980s and 1990s—too late to affect her own education. "Just lucky, I guess," she jokes.

Grandma Marie notices Thomas looking at the words on the pages of her open novel, and she bites her tongue. She has strong feelings about the fact that her grandchildren can't read or write, but, after numerous heated conversations with Kathy urging her to introduce the children to reading and writing, Grandma Marie has decided to let the issue drop—at least for now.

After lunch, Kathy and Thomas say goodbye to Grandma Marie. Kathy drops Thomas off at the swimming pool and goes home for a bicycle ride around her neighborhood.

At ⌐ I. I ⌐..⌐ , Thomas, his friend TaShawn, and TaShawn's father, who picked the boys up at the pool, walk in the door. Thomas asks Kathy if TaShawn can stay for dinner, spend the night, and log onto school with Thomas in the morning. Kathy agrees. TaShawn's dad is just on his way out the door when Mary Beth breezes in. As Kathy, Mary Beth, and Thomas prepare dinner, Mary Beth entertains her family and TaShawn with stories about the animals and plants she and her friends cared for at Nature Preserve Park.

Mary Beth has always loved nature and natural things, which is why she took her old-style acoustic hand drum to the park. She describes how she jammed for hours with her friends, some of them playing acoustic instruments while others, wearing electrode-filled headbands, made music by mind-playing their thoughts and feelings.

Dinner is followed by the usual ten minutes of clean-up chores around the apartment: putting dinner dishes and soiled clothes into their respective ultrasound machines, telling the robot vacuum units to clean the floors and carpets, voice-activating the self-cleaning mechanisms on the showers, toilets, and sinks in the bathrooms, and putting away the piles of clutter. Then Mary Beth heads to her desk VIVO for an evening of college classes, while Thomas and TaShawn play games on Thomas' VIVO.

Kathy spends the last few hours before bedtime in front of her bedroom VIVO's display monitor, first logging onto the Daily Post Access to see what visuals the Daily's visuals editor selected to accompany the "op-ed column" she inputted that morning, then catching the world news and talking to a couple of friends. Finally, she adjusts her VIVO's voice-out speed to a higher WPM (words per minute) setting, turns off the monitor, and spends the last half-hour of her day lying on her bed, eyes closed, listening to a complete longstory—they were called "novels" back in the 20th Century when people still wrote and read them—on one of the many longstory networks.

OK, there you have it. A day in the life of an oral-culture family. It's also a utopian fantasy about a privileged middle-class family living at a time of relative peace and security in an electronically-developed capitalist society in the year 2050.

Based on what our world is like today at the start of the 21st Century, is such a mid-21st Century scenario even remotely possible? Might there really be places on Earth like this place where Kathy, Mary Beth, and Thomas live—communities where life is this pleasant, this free of war, poverty, violence, crime, hate, unemployment, homelessness, hunger, abuse, disease, and environmental destruction? I doubt it.

But I do think that this one-day slice of Kathy's family's life will prove to be accurate in one respect: in the year 2050, in the electronically-developed countries, no one—except perhaps Grandma Marie, a declining number of her fellow book hobbyists, and a handful of linguists, historians, academic "literacists," and archeologists—will be writing or reading. They won't need to—which is why writing and reading are headed toward extinction. To the extent that VIVO technology is now, at the beginning of the 21st Century, rapidly being developed and is almost in place, writing and reading are already *technologically* obsolete and will soon be *functionally* obsolete.

Welcome to the new oral culture of the 21st Century. We're quickly moving—being forced to move by the technologies which we ourselves are creating and setting in motion for this very purpose—into an age of oral-aural communication and information storage and retrieval.

Why do I think there's an oral culture in our future? Look at the clues in our present.

• Billions of people are nonliterate or functionally nonliterate and, therefore, cannot use ordinary text-driven computers—even if they could get hold of them. There is a growing world-wide need and demand for computers that can speak and be spoken to, and there is a computer industry eager to supply that demand.

• Most of the world's nations do not have the enormous resources and/or motivation required to make their populations truly literate.

• For decades, among young people in the industrialized, electronically-developed countries, the amount of writing and reading has declined overall, and young people's literacy skills have either declined or remained extremely low.

• Most young people prefer communicating, storing, and retrieving information orally-aurally and non-text visually, using the full range of electronic devices, from telephones to computers, already available.

• The technology for building effective VIVO computers is almost in place. Research and development of speech recognition, speech synthesis, and speech understanding is soaring as more and more government, corporate, and university research facilities throw their resources into the creation of VIVOs.

• The voice-recognition technology that allows simultaneous translation of spoken languages from one language to another is in place. And the software that translates speech into on-screen 3-D sign language is here.

• McDonald's golden arches, Nike's swoosh, and the hundreds of other traffic, travel, medical, commercial, and informational symbols and icons, understandable to billions of people internationally, are rapidly replacing written words.

• Computer software symbols and icons have become recognizable to today's computer users: Microsoft "Word's" *W*, Apple's ⬛ , diskette and folder icons, Internet smiley symbols :-) and :-(.

• Some watches and clocks with "faces" and "hands" no longer have numerals or timekeeping marks of any kind written on them.

• New voice-activated and voice-controlled electronic devices and appliances, including home and car security systems, home heating and cooling systems, coffee makers, alarm clocks, VCR and DVD players, phone message machines, electronic pocket-sized organizers and datebooks, and phone calling-cards are flowing into the marketplace. They're being joined by:

• The flood of new electronic devices and appliances that can speak back to us.

• The zooming number of magazines, newspapers, and books available on audiocassettes, on CDs, and digitally online using voice-recognition technology.

• The new mobile/wireless digital telephony, voice portals, VoiceXML (Voice eXtensible Markup Language)—the vocal equivalent of HTML (HyperText Markup Language)—and phone-casting, modeled on TV-radio broadcasting, a media network of Internet audio channels available to any telephone.

• WAP (wireless application protocol) allows users to browse the World Wide Web by speaking into cellular phones and other mobile devices. Faster radio-driven applications already threaten to replace WAP.

• Voice-controlled "infotainment" systems in cars and trucks with links to the Internet.

• Singer/entertainer Prince who temporarily replaced his name with a single written glyph, leaving his fans wondering what to call him.

• The tattoos, piercings, scarifications, graffiti tags, and similar graphic symbols that many people in electronically-developed countries are displaying as expressions of their identities.

• The counterpersons at fast-food restaurants who take orders by punching keys bearing pictures of, rather than the words for, Big Macs, large fries, and medium Cokes.

• The restaurant waitpersons who use handheld computers to punch in coded symbols indicating customers' orders to the chefs and bartenders. Their computers also calculate the bill—and the tip.

• The POS (point of sale) computers that are beginning to replace supermarket checkers.

• The huge worldwide popularity of rap and hip-hop, and the growing audiences for other types of spoken-word and performance poetry.

• Electronic books: a mere step away from electronic talking "books."

• Voice-driven e-mail has arrived and has started to replace written e-mail. Finally, chat rooms where people really chat.

• The electronic dog and cat doors that open by being activated only by a particular animal's voice. And the electronic people doors at offices and elevators that open only to a particular human's voice. Voiceprints: we are what we speak.

To paraphrase a line from Bob Dylan's "Subterranean Homesick Blues": you don't need a weather man to know which way readin' 'n' writin's blowin'.

PART I

The End of
Writing, Reading,
and Written Language/Text

Last Writes: Previewing the Reasons Why Written Language/Text Will Become Obsolete by 2050

T he 20th Century is behind us, the new millennium has arrived, and, in the electronically-developed countries:

- most people would rather talk to someone on the telephone than write to them;
- most people would rather watch TV than read a book;
- most schools are experiencing a decline in student literacy skills—a true literacy crisis—with little hope for a breakthrough.

Why is all this happening now? Superficial explanations—such as blaming it on TV, on people's mental laziness or backwardness, or on the schools—simply won't do. Something much deeper, and more difficult to see, is going on.

The growing feelings of alienation from writing and reading, which school children and people of all ages are experiencing and expressing through their day-to-day behavior, are signs and

symptoms of a profound historical, social, technological, and evolutionary change. They are symptomatic of a massive shift that is
taking place: away from the use of written language and back to
the use of spoken language to communicate, store, and retrieve
information in our daily lives.

In the electronically-developed countries, we're witnessing
nothing less than the abandonment of reading and writing, of
written language/text itself, and, in its place, the recreation of
oral culture. The push to develop voice-recognition technology
and VIVOs—voice-in/voice-out computers that we can talk to
and that can talk back to us—is part of this evolutionary leap.

It truly is evolutionary. Historically, before our human ancestors developed written language, they accessed stored information orally-aurally, by speaking and listening—as well as by
seeing, smelling, tasting, and touching. They relied on their
memories to store information that they heard—as well as saw,
smelled, tasted, and touched—and they retrieved it for others
by speaking and acting.

Six thousand to ten thousand years ago, people's memories
were no longer efficient and reliable enough to store and retrieve
the influx of new information that arose with the onset of the
agricultural revolution. To transcend their memories' limits, our
ancestors came up with a remarkable solution: written language.

It was a feat that required great imagination and complexity
of thought and, in today's terms, involved the creation of: new
software—pictographs and alphabets forming written languages;
new hardware or the adaptation of old hardware to new tasks—
pens, pencils, brushes, knives, chisels, inks, chalk, pigments,
animal skins, paper, leaves, wood, stone; and new operations—
writing and reading. Using this new technology, our ancestors
freed themselves from the limits of human memory. Written

language enabled them to freeze and thaw as much information as their hardware allowed.

Today, we in the electronically-developed countries view writing and reading as one of the necessities of human existence, as something we can't do without, like water, food, and sleep. This may be the view we see through our culturally-biased, pro-text eyeglasses, but it's just plain wrong. Not only is written language not necessary to human existence, but we could have reached today's level of information storage-retrieval without ever having created written language in the first place.

If some early society had found or carved a wooden, bone, or stone cylinder, coated it with beeswax, attached a porcupine quill to a hollow gourd, let the quill rest on the wax-coated cylinder, and spoken into the gourd while rotating the cylinder, written language might never have happened. Humanity might have gone right from storing and retrieving speech-based information by memory to doing it by phonograph without entering the world of print culture at all. Humanity's First Golden Age of oral culture might never have ended.

I'm overdramatizing this point somewhat to help lay the groundwork for a different view of written language. Throughout this book, I characterize written language as a technology, a technological solution to specific information-storage-retrieval problems that people faced at a specific moment in history 6,000 to 10,000 years ago. Like most technologies, written language will serve its function until some better technology comes along to replace it. Written language isn't an eternal verity. We can admire it, but we shouldn't worship it.

With written language about to make its exit, and its replacement already stepping through our front door, it is vital that we see written language clearly for what it is: a transitory technology. This reality-check will help us prepare ourselves to say "goodbye" to it and to welcome back its replacement: our old friend, spoken language.

Unlike written language, spoken language—by which I mean speech itself—wasn't/isn't a technology devised by people to overcome human limitations in the face of social and environmental changes. In this sense, spoken language isn't a technology at all. Though we humans created or devised particular spoken languages, we didn't create or devise spoken language itself any more than we created our circulatory systems.

Our ability to speak language is an inborn characteristic of our species. We carry in our genes and our brains the capacity for spoken language. If the day ever arrives that we wave a final "goodbye" to spoken language—and to the sign languages used by people with hearing and/or speaking disabilities—we'll be waving "goodbye" to the species of human beings that we are.

In contrast to written language, spoken and sign languages are "user friendly." As very young children, we just start understanding them and speaking or signing them. We don't have to spend years in school learning to speak. Nor does spoken language drive a wedge into a particular linguistic community the way written language does—dividing its population into those who can read and write and those who can't. Everyone who is mentally and physically able can speak a language.

Historically, spoken language came—and had to come—to humans before written language. Biologically, speech or sign language comes—and has to come—to each child before literacy. This is because written languages are symbolic representations of spoken languages. Had we no spoken language, we could not have created written language. Written language may have emerged as the primary method used to store and retrieve information in certain areas of the world, but it is based on and derived from spoken language.

In the 21st Century, people with access to VIVO-computer technology will once again be able to use spoken language to access all stored information. Talking computers are going to make writing, reading, spelling, alphabets, punctuation, written numerals, and even note-based music notation obsolete.

The obituary for written language won't be written. It will be spoken by someone talking to a VIVO computer in 2050.

Since the mid-19th Century, humanity has been waging a furious assault against written language. This has taken the form of people inventing and developing devices which use spoken language, rather than written language, to communicate, store, and retrieve information. A cornucopia of speech-based devices now exists which has simplified and sped up—and/or completely redefined—the tasks we formerly assigned to text and text-based devices. For the past 125 years, these speech-based devices have been relentlessly usurping the functions of the text-based devices.

The letter, the magazine, the newspaper, the broadside, the book, the flyer, the written advertisement, the memo or written message, the file, the written record, the official document, the written school exercise—all have come under attack. In some cases, direct or instantaneous oral-aural communication devices (telephone, telegraph, live radio, live television) have been doing the usurping. In other cases, devices which store information in the form of speech (phonograph, audiocassette, compact disc, "talkie" movie film, videocassette/DVD) have been responsible.

Since 1990, our minds and resources have turned to the development of talking computers. In our rush to create VIVOs, we're continuing the process Edison, Morse, Tesla, Bell, and their counterparts began.

E-mail appears to be an exception to the above: a form of written message whose popularity is surging in the electronically-developed countries. However, today we are already able to send and receive spoken e-mail, and, given this option, I predict that most of us will soon start speaking our messages instead of typing them. Goodbye e-mail; hello e-talk!

Why have we been so obsessed with researching and developing oral-aural replacements for written language? Because biologically, psychologically, and technologically, we have again hit limits on the efficiency and reliability of our main method for freezing and thawing information.

Formerly, as I mentioned above, it was the limits of human memory to retain the influx of information during the agricultural revolution that led people to create written language. For the last 125 years, it has been the *limits of written language use* that have driven people to seek and develop oral-aural replacements. I'll return to these limits in a moment.

Even though the scientific sector has been working overtime these past 125 years to develop oral-aural and non-text visual technologies, from the wax-cylinder phonograph to the talking computer, the true nature of this process and its goal— to supersede written language's limits by returning to oral-aural methods of information communication and storage—has been largely *undeclared, unacknowledged, and unconscious,* even among the chief developers themselves.

This book has, as one of its main objectives, to acknowledge this process and to raise it to the level of consciousness and awareness. If we understand what is happening and why, we'll be better able to evaluate it and direct its course.

VIVOs will be the last nail in written language's coffin. By making it possible for us to access stored information orally-aurally, talking computers will finally make it possible for us to replace all written language with spoken language. Once again, we'll be able to store and retrieve information simply by talking and listening—and by looking, too, but at graphics, not at text. With this giant step forward into the past, we're about to recreate oral culture on a more efficient and reliable technological foundation.

From a Darwinian perspective, written language is a 6,000-to-10,000-year-old bridge that humanity has been using to walk from our First Golden Age of oral culture to our Second. We undertook this journey to survive as a species. Six thousand to ten thousand years ago, lacking the ability to store and retrieve by memory the growing sum of survival information, our species faced two options: develop new storage-retrieval technology or self-destruct. That's when and why we created the written-language bridge.

As a species, humans have instinctively understood that any systematic failure in our ability to store and retrieve information is a threat to our survival. Now, we in the print-literate nations are instinctively reacting to the fact that written language—our stored-information accessor of choice—has hit its limits and is failing us.

It is failing us, first, because it is no longer able to do the tasks we created it to do and, second, because too many people are unable to use it. An example of the first: for most literate people, communicating, storing, and retrieving information by writing and reading is still far slower and more tedious than doing it by speaking.

Regarding the second, it's sufficient to remind ourselves that the great majority of the world's people, by conservative estimates 80% of humanity, including many living in the so-called print-literate nations, still can't use written language effectively. Most societies in the world today are still oral cultures, and very few of the world's societies possess either the enormous human and economic resources and/or the political will required to fully train their populations to write and read.

There are two other reasons—also related to evolution and natural selection—that we're leaving written language behind. Both are tied to the fact that we have been carrying out the historical commitment that we, in the print-literate societies, originally made to written language. In doing so, however, we have—largely unaware of our dangerous path—strayed too far away from our innate information-communication-storage-retrieval method: speech. Our genes, nervous systems, muscles, and emotions have been sending us a crisis wake-up call, reminding us of our spoken-language survival mandate and telling us to return to our oral-aural roots, or else.

Or else what? Or else the speech-deficiency based physical and mental illnesses that began to strike the print-literate nations in the 19th Century will continue to spread unchecked. Similar in many ways to the older and better understood sun-, motion-, sleep-, and vitamin-deficiency illnesses, speech-deficiency illnesses grew into a late-20th Century epidemic that continues to thrive in many workplaces and homes today.

In other words, we literate folks read and write too much and don't talk enough, and that lack of talk is making us unhealthy. Think hours every day silently writing and reading text on computer screens and on paper.

Another "or else": we print-literates, because of the very activity of our having learned to read and write, have lost that vital unified human consciousness possessed by young children and citizens of oral cultures. Our sense organs have lost their natural ability to work together with each other and with our brains and central nervous systems. As a result, we aren't able to perceive and think accurately about the dynamic reality around us. When we perform actions based on our perceptions and thoughts, it's no surprise that we're often way off the mark.

To be specific, as we learn to read and write, one sense-perceptual activity, the visual, gets separated out from our innate, unified mental-neural-sensory network and gets trained on a non-dynamic reality, text. This leaves us literates with a fractured consciousness, lacking what ancient philosophers referred to as genuine "common sense."

As a result, we struggle impossibly to "make sense" of our universe and our lives. VIVOs, by propelling us forward into oral culture, will help to reintegrate our visuality with our other sense organs and mental-neural apparatuses, thereby restoring our consciousnesses and radically reconfiguring the ways we perceive and think about—and act upon—everything.

Since the late-1800s, we in the print-literate nations have been acting swiftly and positively—though mainly unconsciously—to deal with these crises. We've been heeding the evolutionary mandate of our human physiology and psychology to reverse the widening gap between our present print-oriented selves and our innate, biogenetic, oral-aural selves.

It seems clear to me that the steps we have been taking to stem our speech-deficiency epidemic and to heal our fractured consciousnesses include phasing in speech-based and graphics-based devices, including today's digital voice-recognition technology, while phasing out writing and reading entirely. How else to explain our desperate embrace of the telephone, phonograph, radio, TV, and computer sound and graphics.

On some unconscious mental level, we now seem to understand or believe that talking computers, too, will help us to achieve the wellness and wholeness we seek. We seem to unconsciously understand that hooking ourselves up to these talking-computer I.V. units—IntraVIVOs?—will rid us of textual toxicity and pump us full of lifesaving orality. I am overdramatizing again, but only a bit.

Located at the far end of the written-language bridge, the Second Golden Age of oral culture has been visible to us since the invention of the phonograph in 1877. We trekked the bridge toward our destination decade after decade through the 20th Century. By mid-21st Century, we will finally reach the bridge's end and step off into the future. Once across, we will never look back.

School children's declining literacy rate is a symptom of these deeper processes. As a group, young people in the electronically-developed countries have chosen oral-aural and non-print visual technologies—video, stereo, radio, film, telephone, and computer—as their preferred methods for accessing "live" and stored information.

These technologies, like written language, are external extensions of our brains' memory banks and our sense organs—mindparts located outside of our heads. But unlike written language, they allow us to communicate in the way that's most basic and familiar to us: through spoken language.

Most young people today instinctively understand this rock-bottomness of speech/spoken language. They are in touch with it. They feel it in their bones, their brains, their genes. Why should they read and write, so many young people ask, when they can listen and speak? They view the rules of writing as they view all rules imposed on them by adult society—as devices to dominate and control young people. And they're rebelling.

Students' refusal to go along with the program is causing our schools to develop a record of failure, as each twelfth-, eighth-, or third-grade class graduates with a weaker grasp of reading and writing than the same-grade class of the previous year. Writing teachers are feeling discouraged and demoralized, and many have basically given up trying to teach it. The result: a downward spiral of writing-reading skills and stagnating test scores that became the school literacy crisis of the 1990s and that continues today.

By 2050, if large numbers of students will have been able to gain access to talking computers, all this negativity and failure concerning writing and reading will be a distant memory. All education in the electronically-developed countries will be oral-aural and non-text visual. Students will use talking computers with optional monitors displaying icons, graphics, and visuals to freeze and thaw information.

Instead of the "three R's"—reading, 'riting, and 'rithmetic—students will focus on the "four C's"—critical thinking, creative thinking, compspeak (accessing information using VIVOs) , and calculators. I call it VIVOlutionary learning.

We won't have to wait until 2050. Today, a student assigned to write an essay is able to speak it into voice-recognition software, use their computer's paragraph-check, grammar-check, and spell-check to organize and correct it, "proofread" it by listening to the computer repeat it back, print it out, and submit it to the teacher for a grade. All done using only today's infancy-level software. Tomorrow, and in the tomorrows after that, this process will continue to grow faster, simpler, and more accurate.

The student mentioned above will have proven two things today about talking computers tomorrow. First, that any person—nonliterate as well as literate—with a talking computer will be able to produce a perfect written essay. Second, that *because* any person with a talking computer will be able to produce a perfect written essay, written language will have become obsolete.

Why should the student in the above example bother to print out a copy of the essay? Why should they bother with that final step of translating their spoken ideas into written language? Their teacher certainly doesn't need a written record of their ideas. Using their own voice-recognition software today—or VIVO tomorrow—the teacher is able to listen to the student's spoken ideas online and respond accordingly. Neither the student nor the teacher needs to write anything down in order for learning to occur and for education to take place.

In this scenario, the student and teacher are using their voice-recognition software exactly the way it is supposed to be used. Isn't that *why* we're developing VIVOs? Isn't that what they're *for*? Don't we *want* students to be able to input their ideas orally online and teachers to be able to access those ideas aurally? Voice-in, voice-out: simple.

We developed written language to store and retrieve information, and we are developing talking computers to perform the very same function. Because talking computers will do it more easily, quickly, efficiently, universally, and (ultimately) cheaply, they will replace written language. Simple.

We used to cut our grass with a scythe; then, we invented the push lawn mower and put the scythe in a museum; then, we invented the gasoline-engine lawn mower and put the push lawn mower in the museum. That's the way technology works, and the way we work with technology: we are forever replacing the old with the new.

In the case of written language, however, we are replacing a technology (written language) with a non-technology (spoken language), but we are giving the non-technology a new technological twist: an electronic echo, a gigantic memory capable of storing and retrieving an almost unlimited amount of information in the form of speech.

Written language was a technology created by our ancestors to help them deal with a specific set of historical needs and conditions in a specific historical period several thousand years ago. Today, we are creating VIVO technology to answer a different set of needs and conditions in our own historical period. Soon we'll be placing written language on the museum wall next to the scythe.

Just as some students today might join a choral group, karate club, or chess club as a pleasurable pastime, some mid-21st Century students might join a literacy club to learn written language for fun. But there will be no compelling reason why they would need to learn to read and write and, therefore, no compelling reason why they should have to learn it—or why their schools should have to teach it. Exit the school literacy crisis.

Not only education but also the arts and, possibly, international relations will be transformed in the shift from print to oral culture.

Imagine the literary arts without written language, and the musical arts without written music: a return to storytelling, spoken poetry, and improvised music.

Imagine international relations without written language: dominant nations would no longer be able to force other nations to read, write, and become educated in the former's "standard" languages—a traditional weapon of cultural domination—and would no longer be able to decide which individuals, in the dominated nations, would be allowed to become literate.

These are just two examples of areas in which VIVOs, or, more accurately, people using VIVOs, will reshape the world in the 21st Century. In this book, I take the viewpoint that *good* results *could possibly* come from the fact that talking computers will soon take over written language's job. Lovers of the written word—and I am one of you—I invite you to give the following ideas a hearing.

The creation of VIVOs will create new *potential opportunities* for people in three areas.

• VIVOs will create new *potential opportunities* for the world's nonliterate and semi-literate people to be able to access—through speech or signing alone—the world's storehouse of information and knowledge. For the first time since the introduction of written language, people's nonliteracy or semi-literacy won't prevent their accessing all stored information.

Pre-VIVO electronic technologies have already actualized similar potential opportunities for millions, maybe billions, of people worldwide. Within a period of about sixty years, a huge amount of information that had been formerly inaccessible, because it had been stored in the form of written language, has become available to people who can't write or read. Radio, video, stereo, film, telephone, and computer have opened up an oral-aural and/or non-text visual universe of stored information for the non-readers and non-writers who have finally been able to gain access to these technologies.

Sixty years isn't a long time. The very existence of written language on Earth for sixty-hundred years or more has profoundly affected and reshaped all cultures and communities—even those that are still oral cultures. Now, even before VIVOs sprout from our wrists and lapels, radio, video, and the rest have been busily, and irreversibly, reshaping global reality once more.

• VIVOs will create new *potential opportunities* for all people, whether literate or not, to instantaneously communicate in all languages with other speakers or information storage units. Using today's "old-fashioned" text-entry computers and text-translator software, a person can communicate in writing with another person who reads and writes another language. The problem is that both people must already be able to read, write, and enter text in at least one language, their own.

Using VIVOs, we won't need to know how to read or write, won't need to be verbally fluent in any language other than our own native language, and won't even need to understand a universal language like Esperanto. VIVO units will allow people around the world to speak easily with one another in their respective native languages, thanks to VIVO's simultaneous speech translation function. Electronic Esperanto!

• VIVOs will create new *potential opportunities* to access stored information for many people who can speak and hear, or sign and see, but whose physical and/or mental disabilities make it difficult or impossible for them to write and/or read.

I've italicized the words "potential opportunity" in these three bullets with good reason. The most that the *birth* of a new technology can possibly achieve is to open potential opportunities for people. These opportunities can only become actualized when people actually gain access to the technology and utilize it.

Here's a familiar example. Since most people in the world can speak and hear, they have the ability to use the telephone. But most of the world's people haven't had access to telephones—and still don't—because of the high cost of service and/or the unavailability of service in their communities. True, the huge jump in the number of wireless cellular-phone users around the globe is starting to redraw this picture. Yet it's also still true that, while the invention of the telephone has opened up the *potential opportunity* for everyone to speak across long distances, and more people are using phones worldwide, a telephone still remains out of reach for the billions of people who haven't been able to get their hands on one.

The birth of a new technology, by itself, can't change anything. People having access to and using the new technology can create change and make history.

For the foreseeable future, which includes the VIVO Age of the 21st Century, the issue will continue to be: who controls the new technology and, therefore, who controls whom. As with all technology, talking-computer hardware and software will be developed, patented, copyrighted, programmed, manufactured, encrypted, sold, bought, leased, used, distributed, and shared—or not shared—by those with the wealth and resources to control these processes.

In my opinion, it would be great if all the nonliterate and semi-literate people around the world could actually start using VIVOs on January 1, 2010 to access the world's databanks. But it would be naive to think this will happen automatically just because the technology itself will exist on January 1, 2010. If people want access to talking computers, if we want to actualize the potential opportunities VIVO technology presents to us, we've got to figure out how to do it…and then do it.

The right to have access to the stored information, the collective knowledge, of our community, our society, and our world is a human right. The ability to read and write, print-literacy, is still the key that opens these information vaults. Yet, billions of people around the world are being denied access to this information because they remain nonliterate or semi-literate. Most of the world's people still haven't received their keys. Literacy has historically been treated as a privilege, rather than a right, by those who hold the master keys—and it's as true today as ever.

Most people in the world haven't even seen a library. If they were able to travel to a library, and if they were able to find its door open to them—for many libraries' doors would not be— they would still find the meanings of the sentences in the books on the library's shelves closed to them.

In this book, I say some negative-sounding things about writing and reading. For example, I say that they are about to become obsolete. This isn't intended as an attack on written language. It's merely an observation, part of a broader analysis presented here. And it's definitely not intended as an attack on, or a demeaning of, people worldwide who are striving to learn to write and read.

I have the greatest respect and admiration for children and adults around the world who are trying to achieve literacy. Today, a person's ability to write and read still raises for them new possibilities of communication, knowledge, social and political involvement, employment, enjoyment, self-esteem, creative expression, and much more.

The analysis presented here, rather than closing the doors of hope on those who lack and/or seek the literacy-key to information, communication, and knowledge, opens these doors wide for them. It says that the same VIVO-computer technology that will make written language obsolete will also create potential opportunities for the billions of nonliterate and semi-literate people throughout the world to tap into the world's store of information—without having to learn to read and write at all.

To all students and all others who wish to read and write, I still say: Go to school! Stay in school! Learn to read and write!

We'll need it in our lifetimes!

I say this because written language isn't going to disappear overnight. It will take time: decades, two or three generations, maybe even a whole century. Yet, its eventual disappearance will be the end of a process that's already well underway.

It is ironic that, with the 21st Century's arrival, oral culture is growing in the print-saturated, electronically-developed countries at the exact moment that many electronically-*un*developed countries are earnestly launching literacy campaigns. The near-future course of literacy development in these latter countries is very difficult to predict. However, in the electronically-developed countries today, we need only to look around to confirm that a massive, rapid, electronically-aided decline in the number of writers-readers has begun.

We're witnessing the beginning of an earthshaking transformation of human society away from print culture toward oral culture. It will occupy and involve the energies of humankind from the beginning to the end of the 21st Century and will surely reshape every field of human activity and human consciousness itself. By 2050, in the electronically-developed countries, the use of written language, of writing and reading, will mainly be a thing of the past.

One hundred years beyond, by 2150, all of the world's communities will again be oral cultures. VIVOs will link all of them—including those we build in space—into a single, oral-aural, information-access network: a true, worldwide oral culture.

There is a book, yet to be written, titled *The Future*, that is already *out of print*.

CHAPTER 2

Grammar-Check, Spell-Check, Speak-Check, Listen-Check: The Technological Reasons for an Oral Culture by 2050–[1]

Musing 1

Imagine you teach writing/composition to college undergraduates, as I do. And imagine you've given a take-home writing assignment to your students. The next class period, you collect the essays, all written on computers, and that night you start to grade them for content, organization of ideas, and language skills (grammar, spelling, punctuation, language use). The first thing you notice—and it's old hat by now—is that no matter how rough the content and organization of the essays, the language skills are perfect. Of course! Students ran their completed essays through grammar-check and spell-check programs before handing them in.

One problem facing you at this point, as the person who is supposed to give feedback on these essays and grade them, is that you don't know whether these students are able to write a grammatically correct sentence. Unless they took the time to compare the essay they first typed into the computer with the essay the computer eventually printed out, *they* don't know either. The point here is: does it matter?

Now imagine it's Year 2010, and you're still teaching writing/composition at the same college, and you've assigned a similar essay. By now, students will have traded in their keyboard-type, text-driven models for VIVO computers. How will this change things?

The main difference is that, before, when students entered their essays via text, they had to have *some* writing skills—they had to be able to write *something* that was correct enough in grammar, spelling, punctuation, and vocabulary to enable the computer to produce the flawless finished product. They also had to have some reading skills to read their sentences as they wrote them. Using VIVO computers, students don't have to have any writing or reading skills at all to produce a perfectly "written" essay.

The student merely speaks into her VIVO computer; her words get organized into complete spoken sentences and paragraphs via her miracle software; non-words, incorrect phrases, and grunts get dropped or replaced with their correct counterparts; spelling and punctuation are irrelevant since the finished product will be oral, not printed; finally, she "proofreads" the outputted "essay" by listening to it and making final corrections. She then emails the e-talk folder to you and, just to be certain you receive it, puts a backup spoken copy onto a diskette which she hands to you the next day.

But, wait. You had assigned a *written* essay; the student had misremembered. Easy enough. Her classroom VIVO, like those of her classmates, is programmed with a speech-to-text option. She flips on her VIVO, prints out a copy of her text after running it through grammar-check and spell-check, and presents to you her now correctly completed written assignment. She still hasn't written or read a single word. Voice-in, voice-out—plus push-a-button print-out.

How do you grade her writing? Again: does it matter? Does it matter that she may not be able to read or write?

It matters to you because you're a writing teacher, you're committed to teaching students how to write better, and you're getting paid to do it. You believe it's still very important for people to learn to write and read, so you've decided to change your teaching techniques. From now on, you won't let your students use their VIVO computers at all for writing assignments. You'll forbid them to use grammar-check and spell-check. You'll make them write their essays by hand in class and pass their inky drafts directly to you.

But why bother? Specifically, why is it important for people to learn to read and write at all if—as your student has proven to you—we already have the technology that has rendered these skills obsolete?

Let's look at a parallel in mathematics. I have a ten-year-old friend, Benita Lopez, who hasn't learned the "times" tables and isn't going to. From first grade, Benita has been trained to do math on her calculator rather than on her fingers or in her head. She thinks memorizing "times" tables, rather than using her calculator, to figure 8x8 and 9x9 is like counting seconds all day rather than using her watch to tell the time. I agree.

The watch example contains another parallel. In this age of digital clocks and watches, there are already millions of young people who depend on digital displays to tell time. They can't tell time by looking at the hands of a clock. Is it important that they learn to read clock faces? I don't think so. Watches and clocks represent the old technology. Many children of the Digital Age have never even heard the words "hands" and "face" applied to timepieces, and when they do, they laugh unbelievingly.

Think of it this way: is it important that we, the generation of adults who were brought up using watches with "hands" and "faces," also be required to learn to read sundials? How many of us have ever used a sundial, or know what the shadow-making pointer in the middle of a sundial is called? Check the bottom of this page for the answer.

My ten-year-old friend, Benita, isn't the only one who thinks it's unnecessary for students to learn the "times" tables and other rules of applied mathematics. Today, students in grade school, high school, and college math classes are routinely required to learn to do arithmetic on calculators. Even the SAT college entrance exams have redesigned their math exams to allow for the use of calculators.

Learning arithmetic today *means* learning three things— one and one-half of which are calculator-related. First, it means learning the basic concepts of addition, subtraction, multiplication, and division—which takes the average first grader about twenty minutes. Second, it means learning how numbers are written—another twenty minutes—and how to push the correct calculator buttons to display the desired numbers—twenty seconds. Third, it means learning which buttons to push in order to actually add, subtract, multiply, and divide the numbers— another twenty seconds.

Yet even though Benita is a wizard at using her calculator to come up with the correct answers to arithmetic problems, some adults who have watched her fingers skate across the buttons

---

[1] It's called a gnomon.

feel uneasy about it. They think that she should still be made to memorize 8x8 and 9x9. My response to them has been: why? Wouldn't this be a huge waste of her time? Isn't this the reason we invented calculators in the first place—so that Benita, and the rest of us, would *not* have to memorize the "times" tables?

No, you might be saying, it wouldn't be a waste of her time. Memorizing the rules of arithmetic would help Benita to learn to think and reason. It would be good mental practice for her. And besides, she'll never know when her calculator's batteries might give out or when she might get stranded on a desert island without her calculator and need to know 8x8 and 9x9.

Bypassing the batteries-desert island issue, I'll just say that it's not clear to me that memorizing "times" tables *would* be good mental practice or mentally beneficial for Benita. It's an example of rote learning. Learning to add, subtract, multiply, and divide numbers that are presented to her might have a minor role in keeping a few of her brain cells polished. However, it certainly can't be compared to the superior mental benefits of her using critical thinking to explore some of the theoretical concepts underlying arithmetic—and then using this understanding, and further critical thinking, to solve mathematical problems. Mathematics is critical thinking with numbers.

Helping Benita and her grade school classmates to learn *when*, in which situations, to multiply rather than divide, subtract, or add would offer them important practice in thinking critically. Helping them to learn *how* to multiply, divide, subtract, or add wouldn't really be about thinking critically, and would be better left to their calculators. Giving them the knowledge and skills to understand and think critically about a concept like "number" and its applications—now, that would benefit them mentally.

Similarly, it isn't clear to me at all that—in the coming age of universal grammar-check, spell-check, and talking computers—memorizing rules of grammar, spelling, and punctuation in order to know how to write will be mentally beneficial to anyone.

Don't confuse our learning our native language's grammar—which is the nexus of innate, creative mental and physical processes together with environmental processes that exists when we first learn to speak our native language—with the memorizing of the grammar rules of written language that takes place in school. It's the latter that is the example of rote learning. Memorizing the written grammar rules for subject-verb agreement may provide modest exercise for our brains, but it doesn't really stretch them.

The question shouldn't be: how much is 8x8? It should be: how can we use what the calculator tells us the product of 8x8 is to help solve the problems of our world? Likewise, the question shouldn't be: what's the rule that guarantees that our verb agrees with our subject? It should be: how do we create thoughts and communicate them to others so that they—our thoughts and words—can help us and others to solve the problems of our world?

The spoken word can do the same work as the written word. The heard word can do the same work as the read word. Reading and writing isn't what's important here; thinking critically and creatively—that is, poetically, scientifically, ethically, politically, musically, artistically, environmentally, communally, self-consciously, common-sensically—and communicating, storing, and retrieving our thoughts is.

But, you may argue, we'd lose something if we didn't read or write anymore. We'd lose the ability to think. Our thinking is tied up with our language; if we lost language, we'd lose thinking.

Yes, our thinking *is* tied up with our language, and if we lost language, we *would* lose thinking—at least as we know it. But who said anything about losing language? I've only suggested that the *reading and writing* of language will be rendered obsolete by today's and tomorrow's electronic technology. Actually, it's yesterday's technology that's the culprit. Blame the phonograph! Language itself certainly won't be rendered obsolete. It will be just as essential for thought and communication as ever.

This recognition is based not only on the advent of VIVO technology, but on another fact: writing and reading aren't simply writing and reading. *They're ways we store and retrieve information.* This is their primary function in human society. VIVOs will allow us to store and retrieve information faster, more accurately, and more efficiently than writing and reading. As with most other technological advances, we'll go with the new and drop the old.

When was the last time you churned your own butter? Or even *ate* butter, for that matter?

Musing 2

Sometimes, however, we seemingly go with the new technology and *don't* drop the old. The car definitely seems to have replaced the horse-drawn carriage in the industrially-developed countries. Yet radio, which many people thought would be replaced by TV in the electronically-developed countries, has survived and appears healthy.

When does a new technology, such as VIVO, replace an older technology, such as text, and when do new and old continue to coexist? What conditions must be present for replacement, or coexistence, to occur?

It's a discussion that gets to the heart of the debate swirling around this book's thesis. While I forecast that VIVOs will replace text in the electronically-developed countries by 2050, others argue that text and voice recognition will continue to coexist in the computers and societies of the future. While I model my view on the car's replacement of the carriage, they model theirs on TV's non-replacement of radio. Who's right?

Those who disagree with my thesis seem to have banked their argument on two points. The first is that written language is so central to survival in our print-literate societies that we can't imagine life without it and won't ever abandon it. Point two is that, in the future, written language will still allow us to do certain information-accessing jobs better than VIVOs will, and that this advantage will guarantee written language's long-term coexistence with voice-recognition software and computer graphics.

In Chapter 6, subtitled "Searching for Information Using Sound and Image but No Text," I wrestle with this second point in very specific terms, arguing that, in fact, VIVOs will do those certain information-accessing jobs better than text will. For the remainder of this chapter, I want to address the two critique points above in a more general, overall way. Along the way, I hope we can gain some insight into the nature of technologies and how they evolve, and also into some of the ways people, rightly or wrongly, think and talk about both familiar and new technologies.

Some people, as I said in Chapter 1, think that written language/text has become as basic, irreplaceable, and necessary to our survival as food, water, and sleep. I'll explain why I disagree.

Let's begin by creating a couple of concept-tools to work with. We'll call an activity that every human society needs in order to survive a *basic survival activity*. Eating, drinking, sleeping, finding shelter and/or clothing, reproducing, transporting ourselves, and communicating information are some basic survival activities.

There's a lot of room for discussion here. I think that creating music, song, dance, theater, visual arts, poetry, stories, ritual, science, mathematics, and engineering fall into this category. You may disagree with some of these, and you may want to join me in adding others. Importantly for this discussion, I want to add *storing and retrieving information* to this list.

A second concept-tool: let's call any activity that exemplifies the primary way a specific society carries out one of these basic survival activities a *culture-based essential* of that society.

Take shelter and/or clothing, for example. The primary way this basic survival activity is exemplified in the industrialized countries is that most of us —with the exception of some homeless and/or very poor people—live within some kinds of structures or buildings and wear clothes that cover most of our bodies and protect the soles of our feet. There are other societies that do not shelter and/or clothe themselves in these ways.

For most people in industrialized countries, then, living in buildings and wearing clothes and footwear are culture-based essentials. This may change with global warming, new technological advances, new attitudes towards nudity, and so on, but for now, buildings and clothes are essential to us. The categories of basic survival activities don't change over time; the culture-based essentials of a society are always changing.

Now, let's put these tools to work. Some people I've talked to about the thesis of this book get very upset. Writing/reading, they say, is here to stay. VIVO computers will not replace text in print-literate cultures because text has become basic to our survival as a species. We depend so much on written language to communicate, that giving it up is an unthinkable option.

I think they're wrong. They're confusing writing/reading as a basic human survival activity—which it isn't, and has never been—with writing/reading as a culture-based essential of a handful of societies around the world—which it has been for centuries but won't be for much longer.

Information storage and retrieval, not writing and reading, is the basic survival activity. Writing and reading has just been the primary way—the culture-based essential method by which— we've stored and retrieved information in the print-literate countries. This doesn't mean that most people in these countries are functionally literate. It means that it has been via the *written* word that those who control information in these countries have primarily chosen to freeze and thaw information.

Now writing and reading are about to be rendered passé by a new culture-based essential: VIVO technology. We can continue to read and write, or we can learn to read and write, but we won't *have to* in order to store and retrieve information or to participate in the full range of our society's basic survival activities and culture-based essentials.

It's worth noting here that, when an established culture-based essential of a society gets replaced by a new one, this usually creates a domino effect, causing other culture-based essentials of that society to be replaced as well. For example, VIVOs will cause the familiar notes-on-staff written music notation—a culture-based essential method of storing musical information in some Western societies—to get bumped in favor of new—and ancient—notational and non-notational methods.

Even if I were able to get my critics to agree that text is just a culture-based essential rather than a basic survival activity and, as such, is potentially replaceable, they would still declare that text will forever coexist with voice-recognition technology and computer graphics. Imagine the frustration, they would say, of trying to scan and skim by ear your VIVO's aural output for a particular piece of information. Text's ability to be easily skimmed and scanned is an advantage that will guarantee text's staying power as a culture-based co-essential alongside VIVOs. We will continue to use text, they would argue, because it's a better technology than VIVOs will ever be for locating information.

But what does being "better" at a job mean as applied to technologies?

Lots of considerations enter here, including how we think about and define a technology and its functions, how much we really understand about it and about its relation to other technologies, how we rank its functions in order of importance, how we view its impact on our health, environment, and culture, and how we talk about the technology and its functions—what words we use to name it and to describe what it does.

Does a car do a better job than a horse-drawn carriage? We need to ask, "At what?" Certainly, a car does a better job of hauling people and things around on land at high speeds. Since this function has superseded, at least in our fast-paced society, any other function that both car and carriage are capable of, it seems true to say that the car does a better job than the carriage.

There are some jobs, however, that carriages still do better than cars—*especially* in industrially-developed societies. Carriages excel at driving lovers slowly around moonlit city parks and on moonlit country hayrides.

Are these romantic carriage rides still a culture-based essential of our society? OK, there's room for debate here. But if they are, they're an exemplification not of the basic survival activity of transporting ourselves, but of some other basic survival activity: part of the mating ritual, perhaps.

Carriages are definitely no longer the primary way we transport ourselves to reach food, water, a place to sleep, a place to mate, a place to earn money, a place of shelter, a place to buy clothes or to get medical help. No matter how cozy and moon-lit those carriage rides may be, they haven't stopped the car from replacing the carriage as our culture's essential method for trans-porting ourselves.

We believe that cars are better than carriages, in spite of the damage cars do to the global environment and to the lives and health of living creatures—factors which our industrial societ-ies have obviously ranked below our need to transport ourselves quickly and efficiently.

Before the invention of the steam and gasoline engines, wouldn't these same societies have sworn that the horse-drawn carriage was "better" than the alternatives of its time, and that it would be around forever as our preferred transporter—the quick-est, most efficient, most impossible to imagine life without, irre-placeable, as necessary as food, water, and sleep? Sound familiar?

Then, the new engine technologies came along, the vision-aries built their automobile prototypes and got them onto the roads, and—though not without a struggle—people slowly be-gan to reject any necessary link between our basic survival need to transport ourselves and our need for horse-drawn carriages.

Although agreeing that we have definitely replaced the car-riage, my colleagues love to point out that TV still hasn't replaced radio. For these colleagues, the TV-radio example proves that not all technologies are necessarily going to get replaced, and it opens the door to the possibility that some older technologies—such as radio and written language—can and will endure.

Are my colleagues correct here? Why hasn't TV replaced radio? My view is that, from the beginning, the prediction itself was over-simplistic and, therefore, flawed. Those who predicted that TV would eclipse radio didn't see that radio's aural-only function would give it certain user-friendly advantages over TV's visual-aural function in certain key situations.

True, families in the electronically-developed countries no longer stop what they're doing and huddle around the radio to tune into the day's vital news or the Jack Benny show. For most families today, it's the TV, the couch, the remote, the chips. But if they want to slice a bushel of apples, jog along the lake, or drive their car (or carriage) to work, radio rules.

TV hasn't eclipsed radio because, although in the broadest sense they do the same job—communicate information—they do it differently, and this difference gives radio the advantage in contexts where we're not able to view a TV screen. How long TV and radio will coexist is still an open question, but for the foreseeable future, they'll continue to compete for our attention.

The introduction of the portable Walkman radio encouraged some couch jockeys to leave their TVs and start jogging by the lake, while the portable treadmill exerciser encouraged some lake joggers to come back indoors and watch TV while they walked. TV and radio, as we know them, will morph through innumerable changes in the years to come, but some variations of visual-aural and aural-only communication technologies will continue to battle it out.

We can draw a useful lesson from this goof in predicting radio's early demise. When a new technology is born, it's often very difficult to predict whether or not it will usurp all the jobs of an existing technology and drive it into obsolescence. We may need a crystal ball to see whether the new and the old, while filling the same very broad job description, may or may not also have some separate functions that will give each an advantage over the other in certain key situations and support their continued coexistence.

In the early 1990s, Dave, a pinball-loving friend of mine,

smugly criticized the forecasters who predicted that videogames would soon eliminate pinball machines. Look, he said, pinball is thriving, pinball manufacturers are still turning them out by the thousands, a new generation of pinball machines has added electronics that make them even cooler, and a new generation of young people is lining up to play them. Dave would have bet anything that pinball would coexist with videogames for a long, long time.

But Dave's optimism couldn't save pinball. To quote from Erik Davis' article, "Game Over" (*Wired Magazine*, February 2000): "...over the last half-dozen years, pinball has been skating on thin ice...increasingly challenged by the commanding might of videogames. And now the ice has cracked. Pinball...is dead.

"After a last-ditch attempt to revive a moribund market, WMS Industries—the Microsoft of pinball—built its last game in November [1999]. Not that WMS has hit the skids. The $375 million Chicago-based company is riding high on slot machines and video-lottery gear, and its stock price practically doubled in 1999. But the pinball division has lost a total of $17.8 million over the last three fiscal years. As far as the bean counters were concerned, pinball was a loser's game—so much so that when Wall Street heard WMS had ditched [pinball]...the company's stock jumped another 6 percent.

"The pinball industry has not completely collapsed. Stern Pinball—a small Melrose Park, Illinois, company recently let go by Sega—will continue to manufacture machines, fulfilling owner Gary Stern's vow to be 'the last man standing.' But Stern is nothing compared with the WMS colossus.... [T]he WMS brands—which over the years have included Williams, Bally, and Midway—accounted for 9 of the 10 top-earning pinball machines in the US...."

How could my friend, Dave, have been so wrong? As so often happens when we try to see what's really happening, he viewed only the moment, rather than the sweep of history. Standing in the calm eye of the videogame hurricane after the storm's leading winds had swept past him, Dave mistakenly assumed that the storm was over and that pinball had survived intact.

"By the late 1980s," Erik Davis writes, "there was a videogame backlash, and pinball was on a roll again, having hybridized old-school flipper action with the emerging world of electronic entertainment. But the writing was on the wall. In 1993, its peak year in the 1990s, WMS estimated the world pinball market to be around 100,000 units; five years later, it cratered to only 15,000 machines."

Dave's affection for the old technology had imprinted in him a wishful-thinking mindset that caused him to mistake pinball's last gasp for a healthy deep breath. It prevented him from understanding that, while videogames and pinball did the same broadly-defined job, videogames would capitalize (literally) on their differences by grabbing the digital advantage and feeding into young people's TV habit. When the trailing winds of the videogame hurricane hit in the late 1990s, both pinball and Dave's wishful thinking were swept away.

When I hear my colleagues predict that text and voice recognition will coexist in 2050, I think of Dave. Filled with affection for the written word and a wish to see it flourish, most of these analysts look only at the present moment for signs that text use is thriving—the surge in written email that began in the 1990's, for example—while ignoring the broader historical trends showing people abandoning text for other technologies. In addition, as I'll discuss in Chapter 6, their view of text's "advantages" over VIVOs is clouded by a wrong model—a text-based model—of how we'll actually use VIVOs to search for information.

Let's wind up this musing about technological evolution by using analogies from handicraft, industry, the visual arts, and the calculator, plus the two concept-tools I defined earlier, to peek further into the future of text.

Today you could learn to make your own shoes. You might enjoy learning to score, cut, punch, and sew up the leather. But for most people in highly industrialized societies, if you don't enjoy it, you don't have to do it. As I mentioned, some homeless and/or very poor people may prove to be exceptions to this example. Generally, however, it's not required that you learn to make your own shoes in order to possess a pair of shoes.

If you continued to enjoy making shoes for yourself and perhaps for your family and a few friends, you'd call it your "hobby." That's what a hobby is: an activity that is non-essential for you in your life, though it might be essential for someone else in their life. If you decided to go into business for yourself handcrafting a small number of shoes for a limited clientele, you'd be practicing a time-honored craft, but your work would still be non-essential to our contemporary society.

The point is, since the production of shoes has been industrialized, handcrafting our own shoes is no longer the way we fulfill this culture-based essential—shoe wearing—of our society. Most of us have *other, easier, more accessible, more feasible options.*

This is what I mean when I say that writing and reading will no longer be culture-based essentials of our society. We will soon have other, easier, more accessible, more feasible options than writing and reading for storing and retrieving information.

Just as there will be people who will continue to make their own shoes, clothes, paper, pottery, home-brewed lager, or casseroles simply for the love of doing it, there will be people who will continue to write and read. But it won't be essential that they do. We're only a few LED flashblinks away (on our digital watches) from that 21st Century moment when it will be absurd to *require* people to learn writing and reading, as our schools do now.

"Not so fast!" you might say. Look at art. Don't people still continue to paint with brush on canvas, even though some artists now use a computer monitor as their "canvas" and a mouse, stylus, or their fingers as their "brush"? Don't we continue to build art institutes to teach painting and museums to exhibit paintings? Haven't we been painting since the dawn of human existence, and don't we imagine that we'll keep on painting until the sun sets on us? Surely, painting and digital art will coexist.

Now, you might continue, aren't we promoting reading and writing in the same way? Aren't there more books being published, more people learning to write and read worldwide, more people typing on computer keyboards and reading computer monitors, more people writing e-mail messages on the Internet, more business and personal letters being written than ever before? Won't we continue to write and read just as we'll continue to paint, despite the new technologies?

Let's backtrack a minute. I believe *creating visual arts* is a basic survival activity of human society. Painting, as one primary way we have created visual arts in our society for thousands of years, has been a culture-based essential, not a basic survival activity.

However, the visual arts are changing, too. Painting with paint on surfaces is probably on the way out. Thousands of would-be artists are forsaking the brush and palette in favor of studying computer art and design at their high schools and colleges, or at one of the hundreds of new multi-media institutes. Many of these young artists have never even touched a paintbrush. Digital art and holograms "painted" with laser beams offer today's artists new options that, in my opinion, are already threatening to make painting yesterday's medium.

If painting disappears, other methods of creating visual art will take its place and become essential in our society. That is because visual artists must communicate in visual terms; they have no other option.

Similarly, if writing and reading disappear, other methods for storing and retrieving information will take their place and become essential in our society. What other methods, what other options, will we have? Our best option: instead of writing it, we'll speak it, sign it, and/or present graphics of it to our VIVOs; instead of reading it, we'll listen to it, view sign language of it, and/or view graphics of it through our VIVOs.

I've mentioned that basic survival activities endure, while their concrete manifestations, the culture-based essentials of specific societies, are ever-changing. Painting itself used to have, among its many social functions, an essential *information storage* function, which it no longer has in electronically-developed societies.

Many pre-literate era paintings, for example cave paintings, recorded events—"the news," as we call it—for other people (or perhaps for gods, ancestors, or other living creatures) to see. The painting said a battle occurred in a certain location and a certain number of people were killed, or a hunt resulted in three bears killed, or an eclipse of the sun occurred at a certain time. Some paintings recorded *future* "news"; their artists believed that painting pictures of wished-for future events would cause the events to happen.

More recently, many paintings continued to record "the news." Think of the 18th and 19th Century paintings of Indigenous Peoples of the Americas which were done for the purpose of recording their looks, dress, customs, and cultures for Europeans of that time. Today, photography, movies, video, and computer graphics have usurped painting's function of creating a visual record of the news.

Few instances are left where painting or drawing is essential—offers the best option—for visually recording events in our electronically-developed societies. One example is that of the courtroom artist whose sketches of courtroom events, when cameras are banned, usually provide the only visual record for people outside the courtroom. However, with TV cameras becoming ever more present in courtrooms, I wouldn't advise anyone today to plan a career as a courtroom artist.

We've said "goodbye" to the once-essential "record-the-news" function of painting, and we're getting ready to say "goodbye" to the once-essential "record-the-news"/information storage-and-retrieval function of writing and reading. Very soon, VIVOs will be reducing writing and reading to a mere *hobby* for every literate person in every electronically-developed society in the world.

These glimpses into the worlds of handicrafts and art provide a further insight into the evolution and eventual replacement of written-language technology. While a few people in electronically-developed societies may still be handcrafting their own shoes, most aren't—and can't. As a society, we're no longer adept at that technology, just as many young artists today are no longer adept at the technology of applying paints to create visual art. Technologies, even culture-based essential technologies, come and go; no technology is immune.

That's why we're pausing here for a moment to thank, salute, and prepare to say "goodbye" to another old friend, one much cherished by lovers of the technology we call text: skimming.

Most experienced readers have developed this ability to skim a page at high speed in search of textual information. Our eyes can dart up, down, and around—a wonderfully quick and efficient method both for locating information that we already know is there and for discovering new information. Why would we ever want to say "goodbye" to this magnificent ocular search engine? What "better" technology could ever replace it? Colleagues who disagree with this book's thesis frequently pose these rhetorical questions.

My reply is that we're saying "goodbye" to skimming because, as with handcrafting shoes today and painting art tomorrow, people in the electronically-developed countries at mid-21st Century won't be able to do it. It won't matter that skimming is a magnificent skill—which it is! History is littered with magnificent skills and technologies that we, in the industrially- and electronically-developed countries, have cast off and replaced with newer ones.

Recognizing medicinal herbs in the wild and using them to cure illness, building a dugout canoe, tracking animals, scything grass, predicting tomorrow's weather, yes, even skillfully driving a horse-drawn carriage: lost arts, lost crafts, lost skills, lost technologies. At one time, dynamic culture-based essentials of thriving societies; now, mere exhibits in our natural history e-museums.

In place of visually skimming text in the VIVO Age, we will aurally "skim" VIVO output using our enhanced 21st Century auditory skills. In fact, we're already using primitive aural-skimming skills today when we fast-forward scroll through our telephone answering-machine or voice-mail messages listening for particularly interesting bits of talk, when we interrupt a speaker to ask about something they've said, or when we use our voice-recognition software to <Find> a piece of voice-out that we heard five minutes ago.

However, aural skimming is a different animal from visual skimming. A page of text has spatial dimensions; by providing a static visual field with definite boundaries, the page allows us to seamlessly skim text that we've already read, together with text that we haven't yet read. Listening involves surfing a dynamic (not static), temporal (not spatial) wave of sound with indefinite boundaries.

There is no precise parallel, no exact fit, to textual skimming in the listener's world. However, the assumption that there *should* be—the reliance on an incorrect model which proclaims textual skimming to be the standard and then demands a one-to-one correlation between the features of textual skimming and aural skimming—seems to be at the root of the idea that textual skimming will endure.

The argument goes like this: compare visual and aural skimming, recognize that aural skimming is fundamentally different than visual skimming (spatial vs. temporal, and so on), and conclude that aural skimming is less "better."

Advocates of this argument are taking a wrong approach here, not only because they are using the textual model as the standard for evaluating an aural model, but because they are isolating both types of skimming from their general contexts and attempting to compare their features and merits out of context.

Here's what I mean. Skimming text is just one of dozens of skills involved in using written-language technology. Skimming itself employs a family of other text-related skills. The larger question of whether talking computers will replace written language doesn't hinge just on our answers to narrower sub-questions such as whether skimming text is more efficient than skimming speech.

Both voice-recognition technology and written language are broad, complex technologies, larger than the sum of their parts, and their fingers reach into every area of life in electronically-developed societies. These technologies will stand or fall depending on a multitude of issues: social, cultural, economic, political, biological, psychological, and, of course, technological. To really understand whether written language and VIVOs will coexist, we have to analyze the big pictures—the full contexts, both past and present—of both.

At first, most people referred to the car as a "horse-less carriage." They based their conception of a car on the model of a carriage, and this shaped their often-heated debates about whether cars would ever replace carriages.

Conceiving of a car as a "horse-less carriage" led people to seek one-to-one correlations between the two technologies—to single out a car part or phenomenon, compare it with a carriage part or phenomenon, and use that comparison to decide whether the car could ever supersede the carriage.

Cars were much noisier than carriages, they declared. Gasoline was hard to find, and carriages didn't need it. Car engines, unlike horses, didn't reproduce themselves. A horse and buggy was more affordable than a car. These types of comparisons created almost universal agreement, early in the 20th Century, that the car was a mere gimmick, a wacky contraption that wouldn't seriously threaten the carriage's role as our culture-based essential method of transport.

The very language people used, "horse-less carriage," expressed their naive view that the car was merely a carriage with an engine dropped into it and a horse unhooked from it. Does this sound like the equally naive view that the VIVO will be merely a text-driven computer with more voice-recognition software dropped into it and the keyboard unhooked from it?

People's insistence on viewing the car as a quantitatively altered carriage blinded them to the qualitative leap that was taking place before their eyes. It's a failure that commonly occurs when a new technology arrives.

In the VIVO Age, searching for and accessing stored information will require new conceptual paradigms and new skills. As we continue to interact with our VIVOs, we'll continue to develop aural speech-review methods and software that—if we choose to look at them in that way—may appear somewhat analogous in certain respects to textual skimming. However, by 2050, most people living in e-cultures won't be able to either read or skim and, therefore, won't understand the analogy, won't hold up textual skimming as the golden standard for reviewing information, and definitely won't mourn skimming's loss.

To return to this Musing's broad theme, there's nothing *intrinsically* valuable in reading and writing. They're valuable only so long as they're useful for storing and retrieving information, and their time is about to pass. The technology that will usurp their function and return us to an oral culture is being put into place—by us. The issues that face us now aren't about whether we can reverse this process, because we can't. The issues are political, economic, and moral, and involve how we can use the new technology, and the incredible changes it will bring, to create a better world than we have now.

To illustrate this last thought, let's consider again the calculator-VIVO analogy mentioned above in Musing 1. Think of the effects the calculator, and its non-electronic predecessors, from abacus to adding machine, have had on our world.

Today there are hundreds of thousands, perhaps millions, of retail clerks, supermarket checkers, fast-food and restaurant cashiers and servers, movie theater cashiers, small business owners, and probably some mega-corporation CEOs in the electronically-developed countries who are mathematically nonliterate, but who are successfully working at jobs that require them to manipulate mathematical information—all thanks to the calculator. In the past, these individuals simply would not have been able to do these jobs. By allowing them to tally customers' totals and calculate customers' change—forget the CEOs here—calculators have opened up significant new job possibilities in applied mathematics for the world's workforce.

Ironically, the same calculator technology, that has made arithmetical figuring-in-one's-mind obsolete, has made it possible for everyone who can acquire a calculator—including mathematically nonliterate people—to store and retrieve mathematical information.

Analogously, VIVO technology, which will make writing and reading obsolete, will likewise make it possible for everyone who can acquire a VIVO—including linguistically nonliterate and semi-literate people—to store and retrieve the world's totality of information. Where calculators have been opening the applied-mathematics door, VIVOs will be opening the applied-knowledge door. What could be more political, economic, and moral than that?

Alas, VIVOs will also be making writing/composition teachers like myself as passé as expressway toll-takers, who are rapidly being replaced by laser beams zapping car fender bar codes and dashboard transponders or, more recently, by radio-frequency technology zapping embedded microchips. Puns regarding "for whom the bell tolls" in the classrooms of the future may not be appreciated by my long-suffering, fellow writing teachers.

CHAPTER 3

(Ear)Wax Makes History:
The Technological Reasons
for an Oral Culture by 2050–[2]

Musing 3

J ust as the first simple box camera doomed painting's recording-of-events function to obsolescence, the first wax-cylinder phonograph doomed writing's and reading's storage-and-retrieval-of-information function to the same fate.

Through the course of the 20th Century, we watched these humble, non-electronic devices giving birth to their functional offspring: the phonograph/wax cylinder producing stereo, tape recorder, compact disc player, and—still birthing as we speak—VIVO computer; the camera/film producing movies, video, and computer graphics.

Let's start by discussing the phonograph: VIVO's mom. It was she that will prove to have been mightier than the pen.

Sounds are what spoken language produces. But before the phonograph, sounds couldn't be stored and/or retrieved, except in the memories of living creatures (we're discounting mountain echoes here). A sound not heard and remembered was truly lost. If those who heard the sound forgot it or died, it was beyond retrieval. It is amazing to think that, for millions of years, *until only one-hundred and twenty-five years ago, the brain of living creatures* (think of parrots as well as humans) *was the only device capable of storing and retrieving the transitory sounds of animal and human speech.*

Information storage is as basic to a people's survival as air, food, and water. A society needs to know how to raise and protect its young, survive the elements, choose what to eat and drink, fight disease. It can't spend each day, or even each generation, learning these again from scratch. Experiencing the need to store information for later retrieval, early peoples utilized two processes simultaneously.

First, they spoke to other people, who, hopefully, would stay alive for a while and, hopefully, would remember what had been said and would repeat it correctly to others, who, hopefully, would interpret it correctly, and so on. Second, they drew, carved, chiseled, painted, sculpted, built, wove, and tattooed pictures or objects, which, hopefully, would last for a while and, hopefully, would be interpreted correctly by others.

By combining the two processes, a society succeeded in storing information far beyond the momentary life-span of words spoken into air, sometimes even beyond the life-spans of the speakers and listeners, their offspring, and their society itself. Historically, this combination of processes often proved to be an extremely effective societal survival mechanism. Many of these so-called oral (really oral-aural-visual-olfactory-gustatory-tactile) cultures lasted for thousands of years, and many continue to this day.

Each of these two methods of information storage and

retrieval had its particular shortcomings, as mentioned above. The memory-storage method depended on people's ability to receive, remember, and pass on with accuracy the original information—activities notably vulnerable to human error. The picture-object method depended on the possibility of preserving the pictures and objects from the elements (sun, water, ice, wind, sand) and from destruction by other living creatures—another chancy endeavor. It also depended on the type and amount of drawing space and/or construction materials available.

It was partly due to these general shortcomings or limits, and to the human ability to develop new technologies that can transcend the perceived limits of older technologies, that the processes we label "written languages" arose. Texts based on content (idea, theme), those based on sound (phonetic or "alphabet" type), and those—like Egyptian hieroglyphics—incorporating the two allowed unspoken thoughts and spoken language to be frozen and thawed.

But people's felt need to break through these general limitations doesn't, by itself, explain why written language came about. Today, we can look at contemporary oral cultures and see that, although their oral-aural and picture-object methods of information storage-retrieval suffer from these same aforementioned limits, these cultures persist without text. Even with their limits, these methods work well enough for the types of information today's oral-aural societies use and the types of communication requirements they have.

No, to fully explain the creation of written language, we have to add another ingredient: the rise of a new type of socio-economic system that was generating new types of information and new types of requirements for recording and communicating that information. I'll return to this question in Musing 4.

Written languages also changed the relationship of human memory to information storage. Prior to written languages, the actual spoken word, unable to be stored except in memory, had to travel directly from memory to memory, that is, directly from person (or parrot) to person (or parrot). With the advent of written languages, the spoken word, transformed into the written word, could take an indirect route. People didn't have to talk directly to each other (or to parrots) in order to communicate. Ideas didn't have to be heard in order to be preserved.

Socially-agreed-upon *writing rules* evolved, enabling a society to cluster certain written symbols in certain ways that reflect the sounds, meanings, and grammar rules of its spoken language. Reading was the process of applying the same rules to retrieve what was thought or spoken via the written symbols. The engine for the transformation to written language was society's need to store and retrieve the new types and growing amounts of information more accurately and reliably.

Writing and reading as a technique of information storage and retrieval had its shortcomings as well—most of them stemming from people's misuses of these rules. The writer-to-reader communication would be accurate and reliable only if the writer, hopefully, knew the correct writing rules and symbols and, hopefully, transcribed their own thoughts and/or spoken words correctly, and only if the reader, hopefully, also knew the correct writing rules and symbols and, hopefully, was able to obtain a copy of the written words and read them correctly.

This doesn't even touch on the differences between spoken and written language with respect to the interpretation and communication of *meaning*. Written language lacks voice tonality, facial expression, body language, and the other features that help the listener to understand speech. Nor are we usually able, as readers, to interrupt the writer on the spot, as listeners can interrupt a speaker, to ask what her words mean. Despite these shortcomings, writing and reading mushroomed, among the industrialized nations, into the leading technique for freezing and thawing messages, and, today, most nations profess a 100% literacy rate as a goal.

Then came the phonograph, and the storage-retrieval business has never been, and will never be, the same. Other than displaying its information visually (and therefore aiding people with hearing and speech disabilities), there's no work that writing and reading can do that couldn't be done by a phonograph.

We can all think of examples, like roadside billboards and airplane-pulled advertising banners, whose replacement by loud phonograph/stereo sounds might produce an even worse form of noise pollution than the visual pollution already produced by the former, but that isn't the point. The point is that the phonograph offered a new alternative for storing and retrieving speech and other sounds accurately and reliably. Like writing and reading, it too allowed for indirect human communication with its wax cylinder—or LP, audiocassette, or CD—acting as patient "middleman," the role previously "owned" by the sheet of paper and the roadside billboard.

All the words, though not the pictures, in all the books on all the library shelves could be replaced by audio CDs or "talking" microchips, and it wouldn't make any real difference (except to people with speech and hearing disabilities). In fact, each year more and more people are listening to "books" through their stereo headsets, their car or bedside CD systems, or streaming off the Internet. We have discovered that reading a book requires our looking at the text, while listening to one allows us to do other things—drive to work—at the same time.

The VIVO computer does the same thing for speech storage and retrieval as its forebear, the phonograph, only it does it better. It can freeze a lot more messages in a lot smaller space than a CD can, and it can retrieve them much, much faster.

In 1964, I took a graduate course in linguistics at The Massachusetts Institute of Technology with Professor Noam Chomsky. He made the point that computers would never be able to always translate human speech perfectly into electronic signals because certain words, phrases, and sentences are phonetically ambiguous. The computer wouldn't necessarily be able to tell from the sounds we made which word, phrase, or sentence we formed. Homonyms like bear/bear/bare are the clearest culprits, but phrases and sentences like the old "I scream for ice cream" are easy enough to conjure up.

Chomsky's point is a logical point about the possibility of computers' always guessing right, and he's right. But linguists, philosophers, computer scientists, social scientists, programmers, and other knowledgeable specialists are in the process of tremendously increasing the computer's guess-right to guess-wrong ratio by identifying the phonetic, syntactic, semantic, and social-contextual linguistic rules of human languages, and they've begun programming VIVO computers with these rules. It's starting to happen: computers have begun to translate speech into electronic signals, and vice versa, almost, if not always, perfectly.

Let's look at some of the ways we're already helping our voice-recognition software to "guess right." First, we're *speaking a little differently*. We're trying to avoid the use of phonetically ambiguous speech patterns like "I scream" vs. "ice cream." We're exaggerating the pause between "I" and "scream," and also between "ice" and "cream," in order to not confuse our electronic buddies.

This is nothing new; we've always altered our speech to

accommodate our voice-related technology in order to make it more user-friendly. It's why we try to speak more clearly over the telephone, and why TV/radio announcers and ad people use those bell-like tones. It's why we've developed Seaspeak, the language sailors use to speak from ship to ship by radio: A=Alpha, B=Bravo, C=Charlie, D=Delta, W=Whiskey, X=X-ray, Y=Yankee, Z=Zulu.

A larger problem is to manage words, phrases, and sentences that are phonetically/syntactically/semantically ambiguous no matter *how* we say them. Slang is often like that: "D'Azure's a bad drummer." Does it mean that she's a good drummer or a bad one? Figurative language is also a problem: "She's built a nest for her family." Has she really built a nest for her family, or has she created an especially warm home environment?

Will we stop using slang and figurative language to make life simpler for our VIVOs? Perhaps a bit at first. More likely, we'll be tailoring each VIVO-computer's program to fit the social settings, work requirements, and speech patterns of the person(s) who'll use it, much the way we fill our refrigerator with the foods we want to eat.

I foresee a dual process occurring over time. Early on, we'll alter our speech to help our VIVOs understand us, while our VIVOs will continue to grow more sophisticated at guessing what we're saying. Soon, VIVOs will guess right so much of the time that we'll converse with them as normally as we converse with our friends, and VIVO manufacturers will be confident enough to offer "money-back guarantees" and "full refunds" if their VIVOs goof.

To end this Musing with a smile, it's enlightening to check out how *written* language has shaped the way literate people speak (and write)—our vocabulary—and to speculate how the technology of VIVO-computer voice-outs will both affect these older speech patterns and create new VIVO-"literate" speech patterns in the 21st Century.

Listen to how we print-literates speak: "all of the above," "erase that thought," "scratch that idea," "in order to under-score that point," "quote/unquote," "dot your I's and cross your T's," "entering a new chapter in your life," "lift a page from her life," "are we on the same page here regarding this matter?" "don't write him off; he's got a lot of potential," "I wouldn't rule it out," "no more telling lies, period!" And don't forget the two-fingered quotation marks we "write" in the air with both hands.

Will we still use these phrases and gestures 50 years from now? I doubt it, but even if we will, we will certainly have "erased" their original, script-based meanings from our memories.

What new phrases will the VIVO Age inspire? Perhaps we'll be saying "shout" that idea instead of "underscore" it, or "gag" that idea instead of "scratch" it. How about: "Ruthie, what were you doing 25 BEEPS-AGO?" or "Hurry, Henry, we've got to be at work in ten BUZZES!" (Check Chapter 6 for clues to these formulations.) Or: "Children, I want this room UH-FREE be-fore you go out to play!"—that is, keep it clutter-free, just as you should keep your speech uncluttered with "uh's" when you talk to your VIVO.

Musing 4

The rise of agricultural production—which included the domestication and breeding of animals and the cultivation of plants for food—in ancient times created new pressures to tran-scend the limitations of traditional information storage-retrieval methods. In order to move forward and survive, people in these landbound societies created written language.

The human-memory and picture-object methods of storing and retrieving information were unable to fill the expanding needs of the inhabitants of this new type of economic and social order. These inhabitants created writing and reading as a new technology for accessing new types and amounts of stored information and for communicating these in newly required ways.

Six thousand to ten thousand years ago, some human societies had begun to evolve from nomadic, hunter-gatherer societies into more permanently-landbound, agricultural societies. As a result, they began to generate, store, retrieve, and communicate new types of information.

For the people of most of these new settled communities, private ownership sooner or later became a reality: private ownership of land, water, livestock, edible products grown on the land, timber and other building materials and the shelters and structures built with these, and, finally, other human beings captured and enslaved.

What land and water was owned? How much of it did they own? What were its boundaries? What livestock and produce was owned? How much was produced? How much was promised in trade? How much was received? If the community was further subdivided into clans or families, who owned what land, what animals, what houses, what enslaved people? Who would inherit what property? And how could one settlement's vital, ever-changing, production data be communicated to other settlements located distances away? These were questions that either had never arisen, or had arisen in only very limited ways, within the former nomadic communities.

Hunter-gatherers migrated with the wild herds, their paths and encampments being dictated by the course of their prey and the seasons of the year. For the most part, it was an unchanging routine, one that had characterized the greater part of human history. Community life of hunter-gatherers, based as it was on a migration economy, also remained mostly unchanged through the eons. The young people of the community were taught the eternal lessons of survival and culture—which are inseparable in every age—by being shown and by being told.

In oral-aural communities, much the same information was communicated from one generation to the next. Each new generation of parents and elders repeated the same lessons they had been taught to each new generation of children. The types and amounts of information, the actual lessons, beliefs, and rituals themselves, may have rarely changed.

Also, the conditions and requirements for communicating the information—the language spoken by the person giving the information and the person receiving it, where the information-giver and information-receiver lived in relation to one another, and so on—may also have rarely varied. This is because the life patterns inside nomadic communities rarely varied.

All this changed as some communities opted, or were forced by survival considerations, to settle on the land. Some societies approached land settlement, herding, animal husbandry, and crop harvesting as they had approached hunting and gathering, dividing the produced wealth equally among their members. Most societies, however, experienced the creation of new class divisions, based on private ownership, that hadn't existed before: between those who owned more land and livestock and those who owned less, or between those who owned some and those who owned none.

In these class societies, writing, reading, and written language became a means not only for recording information but for *main-*

taining and strengthening the rule of the dominant classes over the dominated classes, the dominant societies and nations over the dominated societies and nations, and the dominant gender, males, over the dominated gender, females. It remains this way today.

It was the needs of the new power elites, the Haves, of the new agricultural class societies that really drove the development and refinement of written language. It was they who needed written language to inventory their new holdings and record their transactions in order to defend their individual property rights against those who might seek to usurp them. Communal-egalitarian settler societies might have needed written language, too, but not so desperately.

From the moment the first societies containing class divisions appeared, the owners of wealth realized two things. First, in order to remain dominant, they would have to control as much of their societies' information as possible. Second, in order to control the information, they would have to control the methods by which the information was stored and retrieved. This meant that they not only had to develop and refine written languages, but they also had to control them. This need to control the technology for storing and retrieving information gave birth to today's division between literate and nonliterate classes, communities, and nations.

The Haves simply could not let written language fall into the hands of the Have-Nots. They realized—as did some of the Have-Nots—that literacy was the key which the Have-Nots could use to gain access to their societies' information storehouses. Permitting mass literacy was a risk the Haves dared not take. The history of written language is the history of the Haves denying written language—and thus the information conveyed by written language—to the Have-Nots.

CHAPTER 4

Recovering from Scriptitis: The Evolutionary Reasons for an Oral Culture by 2050

Musing 1

Histology will speak of it as a 6,000-to-10,000 year technological and cultural bridge: a bridge whose primary function in human society was to allow us to *recreate our oral culture on a broader and more efficient level.* The "it" here is writing, reading, and written language itself.

Six-to-ten thousand years ago, we began the process of adopting written language as a tool in order to help our oral culture solve an increasingly difficult problem. We were not being able to store and retrieve information in an efficient and reliable way. With the agricultural revolution generating so much new information, we had hit the functional limits of both human memory and picture-object visual aids, which were, at that time, the only two ways we had to store and retrieve information. We needed to find a way to break through.

We adopted written language as a tool for transcending these limits, but only as a *temporary tool* that would, in time, help us reach the point where we could discard it and return to our oral-cultural tradition.

I don't mean that we were conscious or aware 6,000-to-10,000 years ago that we were inventing written language as a mere stopgap—as a short-term measure to temporarily solve the information-storage emergency we were experiencing. We probably had no idea that reading and writing would, over the next 6,000-10,000 years, function so strongly in opposition to orality, that they would take us so far from our oral culture, or that we would ever have to think—as I'm doing right now— about if, when, and how we would ever return to our oral roots. I'm definitely using hindsight here to speculate on our evolutionary needs during that period.

Rather, I mean that, as creatures genetically and psychologically rooted in oral culture, we'll always seek, consciously or unconsciously, to maintain an oral culture or—if we've left it behind—to try to recreate another one for ourselves.

That's what we're doing right now. Since the late 1800's, we, in the electronically-developed countries, have been working furiously to recreate our oral culture. Today, as the 21st Century opens before us, we're taking the final technological step back into oracy: VIVO computers.

For centuries, scientists and engineers have used written language to store and retrieve the data that has made today's research and development of talking computers possible. In this sense, written language—as is true of every technology—has contributed to its own obsolescence. Let written language's obituary show that written language did itself in.

Why are we currently seeing this extraordinary push to develop voice-synthesis, voice-recognition, and voice-understanding capabilities for computers? And why now? I believe that our long-term genetic-strategic human goal of maintaining oral culture is driving the current development of VIVO technology and our imminent return to an oral culture.

Though, in form, a negation and opponent of orality, written language has actually turned out to be our indispensable partner and ally—our technological bridge—that is allowing us to finally reach our long-term goal: to recreate a Second Golden Age of oral culture, oracy's renaissance.

Let's back up a minute and fill in some of the spaces in this broadly sketched thesis. First, our human roots and essence lie in oral culture. Biologically, psychologically, and evolutionarily, humans are spoken-language creatures. Our brains are constructed for this task, and, through our genes, we pass the trait on to our offspring. As human beings, we need to live in an oral culture, to communicate and to access stored information orally-aurally.

Second, we traded spoken language for written language in order to get us through a particular historical crisis. Written language isn't basic to human nature; it's merely a technology we developed. Spoken language, however, isn't a created technology at all. Spoken language, like our lungs that breathe air, our eyes that see colors, and our pelvises that allow us to walk upright, is who we are.

Third, so much time and energy and so many resources have, in the past 125 years, gone into developing non-electronic and electronic technologies which can replace written language's storage-retrieval function, and this process has accelerated with each subsequent decade. I do not believe that this great burst of human effort has happened *merely* to speed up information flow, tighten the power elites' control of global information access, and create new products to sell. A human bio-psycho-evolutionary drive is also at work.

We in the print-literate nations had gotten too far away from using spoken language to store and retrieve information. We were starting to drown in written language. We could feel ourselves losing consciousness—our human consciousness. Sometime in the 19th Century, we received a survival mandate—a wake-up call from our genes and emotions telling us to get our information-accessing act together—and we've been shepherding this project along ever since.

Fourth, we have been no more conscious, since the late 1800's, of this deeper reason for our developing oral-aural, text-replacement devices than were our ancestors, 6,000-to-10,000 years ago, of the deeper reason for their developing written language. In fact, our ancestors created written language for the same reason that we created the phonograph and are creating talking computers: to permit humanity's survival in a world-wide *oral* culture. The only difference is that our ancestors' creation, written language, represents an earlier stage in this "homing" process than do our creations, phonos and VIVOs. But it's one and the same process.

Our genetic and psychological drive to maintain our orality may supply a *general* explanation for the 125-year flood of text-replacement inventions that is culminating in today's frenetic talking-computer development. But there must have been, and has got to be, something else—something more *specific*—that helps to explain why we developed the phonograph 125 years ago and why we're developing the VIVO at this moment in history.

We must have again hit some limits, at least in the electronically-developed countries, on our ability to store and retrieve information using written language. For, just as we created written language thousands of years ago in order to go beyond the limits of memory and picture-object methods of information storage, we must have begun text-replacement R and D 125 years ago, and we must be pushing talking-computer R and D today, in order to go beyond what we've perceived as written language's limits. What are these limits?

1. Writing and reading have become too slow and tedious a method of manipulating stored information.

2. In growing numbers, people just don't want to read and write anymore. Instead they're preferring to rely on the newer oral-aural and non-print visual technologies—telephone, video, stereo, radio, film, and computer graphics/games/voice recognition—to store, retrieve, and communicate information.

3. Too few people, especially in the electronically-developed countries where the need for people to maneuver written data is the greatest, are able to read and write well enough to do the job. The ongoing literacy crisis in our schools offers little evidence, or reason to think, that this situation will turn itself around.

4. Almost all governments around the world lack the resources required to truly train their populations to be functionally literate.

5. Almost all governments around the world also lack the political will to truly train their populations to be functionally literate. They maintain literacy as a privilege for the elite, rather than a right for all, fearing that a literate, better educated citizenry will revolt, threatening the rulers' rule. The result: an estimated four-fifths of the world's population remain functionally nonliterate.

6. Medical issues, physiological and psychotherapeutic, have entered the picture. Immersed in reading and writing for a

third or more of each day, people whose work requires them to keep their noses in their computers, word processors, books, print media, and calculators for long periods of time are getting sick and tired—literally. We're also living longer, and our eyes and carpal tunnels are giving out before our minds are giving out. Our bifocals, trifocals, and wrist splints just don't do much to speed up our writing-reading processes.

It's worth taking some time here to discuss these medical issues, and, to do this, we need to enter the worlds of evolutionary biology, evolutionary psychology, and evolutionary medicine.

Using written language is alienating. As is the case every time we take a deep breath and swim underwater, or type on our keyboards for hours, we prove that humans can adapt to alien—and alienating—environments for limited periods of time. Still, zipping around in an alien medium can take its toll on us physically and mentally.

When we read and write, we're out of our element. It's a different medium than we and our brains were evolutionarily cut out for. Written language uses our eyes and our hands, in silence, and ignores our speech-making and hearing organs. I think it's no different than swimming underwater, which uses our natural breath-holding apparatus but ignores our breathing apparatus. The toll we pay, in both cases, for over-exercising the former to the exclusion of the latter is formidable: we drown.

Another analogy: we're walking-creatures. Genetically, we're not made to sit in one place for long periods of time. We're designed to stand up and walk around fairly frequently to find food, water, and mates.

Research with astronauts has shown that their spending long periods in space sitting relatively motionless inside a tiny space capsule can result in the dangerous buildup of calcium deposits on the soles of their feet. Evolution has fashioned our feet for walking; our feet get ill when all we do is sit. So a gadget has been devised that simulates the effects of walking by repeatedly striking the seated astronauts' soles and preventing calcium deposits from forming on their feet.

But we haven't developed any procedures or technology to help us cope with the prevention and cure of illness caused by our over-inhabiting the alien environment of reading and writing. Sending children to school for thirteen years to learn to read and write is like holding them underwater for thirteen minutes. Maybe that's why so many children rush home to their TV and computer screens after school lets out. They just need to catch their breath from all that enforced silence and written language.

Think of a child who's lying on the living-room floor watching TV after school as a nearly-drowned swimmer sprawled on the beach after being rescued. Or think of that child as engaged in some kind of self-applied physical and occupational therapy. When I was a school kid, we used to run home after school, flop on our beds, turn on our radios, and let The Lone Ranger shoot the calcium deposits off our ears with his silver bullets.

Someone might counter by saying our ability to extend our time in alien environments is *also* an evolutionary adaptive process tied to our survival as a species. They might point out that we've developed scuba technology that allows us to survive underwater, an alien environment, for long periods of time. Therefore, they might argue, we humans have the genetic ability to transform alien environments into non-alien ones. By inventing scuba gear, we've been able to extend our field of movement into another atmosphere. We've made the underwater environment more natural for us, more of our element.

In the future, they might continue, if the surface of the Earth were to become so polluted or filled with nuclear radiation that we couldn't inhabit it, then we could escape to an undersea world filled with the submarine technology that would allow our species to survive there indefinitely. After all, isn't that what the land mammals that evolved into whales, dolphins, and manatees did? And what seals, otters, walruses, and hippos—yes, hippos!—are in the process of doing today?

Over fifty million years ago, the artiodactyl, a land-based ancestor of the whale, was probably able to spend only brief seconds or minutes underwater. But over millions of years, those early artiodactyls gave rise to offspring whose mutated gene structures allowed them to spend more and more time underwater until they evolved into the *whales* we know and love today.

Artiodactyl

Gingerich, P.D. et al. "Origin of Whales from early artiodactyls." *Science* 293 (Sept. 21, 2001) pp 2239-2242. Artist: J. Klausmeyer/*Science*

Completing this analogy, they might ask: couldn't humans be following a parallel evolutionary course with respect to reading and writing? More than 10,000 years ago, humans were the Speaking Creatures. Six-to-ten thousand years ago, having hit the limits of human memory, our ancestors evolved the ability to read and write for short periods before needing to speak and listen again. Today, as a species that needs to access more stored information than ever before in order to survive, we're evolving the ability to read and write for longer and longer periods without doing harm to ourselves. As a result, we humans have become the Speaking-and-Writing Creatures. In the future, who knows? We may evolve into the Writing Creatures, humans with no vocal cords or functioning ears, and twelve fingers on each hand to improve our keyboard technique.

They might also add that while we don't exit the womb writing and reading, we don't exit it speaking either, and that just because a child usually learns spoken language several years earlier than they learn written language, it doesn't *prove* that spoken language is our natural element and that written language isn't.

As a viewpoint to argue against, this is a toughie. But it isn't correct. I think the key to forming a counter-argument is to understand that, from the evolutionary-genetic-psychological point of view, some things that we're able to do are based on other, more fundamental, things we're able to do, and not vice versa.

Let's put our "walkie-talkie" analogy to work again. Consider the following conversation:

Zoe: Humans are naturally walkers. Bipedal walking is etched in bold italics in our genes.

Moe: We're naturally pole-vaulters, too. The fact that we can pole-vault proves that the ability to pole-vault is etched in our genes in as bold italics as is our ability to walk. We are meant to pole-vault just as we are meant to walk. We're in our element with both.

Zoe: I don't think so. Just because humans—some, anyhow—are able to pole-vault doesn't mean that pole-vaulting is one of our defining human characteristics. Walking on two legs, however, is. When children reach age one or one-and-a-half, they just start to walk (unless they have a disability). They don't plan it; they don't necessarily copy anyone's walking behavior; they just start walking, period. If they ever do go on to become pole-vaulters, it was their ability to walk first that made it possible. Pole-vaulting is based on walking, but not vice versa.

(Thank you, Zoe.)

Just as walking is pole-vaulting's foundation, spoken language is written language's foundation. Around age one or two, children just start speaking (unless they too have a disability). Their speech is mind-directed, not just abstracted from experience and spit back. Literacy requires oracy first.

Experience shows that children won't necessarily try to create a written language to store and retrieve information, but they will necessarily try to develop a spoken language—or even a sign language of some kind if they aren't able to speak and/or hear.

Our genes haven't evolved into written-language determinants yet. In fact, our genes today seem to be moving us in the opposite direction: reminding us that our overly-long visits to the alienating atmosphere of written language are not truly "us," and driving us to invent and develop more and more powerful oral-aural methods of accessing stored information.

True, most children feel an initial rush of excitement when they begin learning to read and write their ABCs. They find it fascinating—like playing a game or being let in on someone else's secret code.

A child's first experiences reading words, or watching words appear on the page as they write them, can be compared to a child's pleasure in drawing a picture with milk on a piece of white paper, then heating the paper over a flame and watching the invisible picture reappear in brown. It's like magic.

But this first wave of excitement quickly subsides when

children realize that writing and reading is the name of the game for thirteen years of school, plus college, plus job: a lifetime commitment to an alien practice. And they rebel.

Why *shouldn't* they rebel? Humans are creatures genetically and psychologically designed for oral culture. It's our shtick. As a species—though this or that individual person may prove an exception to the rule—we're more comfortable speaking out loud than reading and writing in silence, even if we have to choose a nonhuman partner—a VIVO computer, for example— to speak with.

The conversations between the starships' crews and their talking computers in the *Star Trek* TV shows and films give us a taste of this process's potential, though *Star Trek* scripts have often seemed to make a point of the various crews' frustrations with not being able to communicate smoothly with their VIVOs. In 370 years, when we reach their star-date and become real Star Trekkers ourselves, will we still be wrestling with our on-board VIVOs over issues of communication and meaning? Probably so.

I want, briefly, in these last few paragraphs, to emphasize the possible harmful physiological and psychological effects of our writing and reading for extended periods.

Our psycho-biological need to live and work in an oral-aural environment remains unfulfilled today for many people in electronically-developed countries. More and more, people are manipulating information in the form of written language as their primary jobs. Many of them come home from work and read and write even more: they read newspapers and novels, surf the Internet, pay bills, write letters or e-mail, figure taxes, create resumes. From the standpoint of evolutionary medicine and psychotherapy, they may be developing an oral-aural deficiency. They may actually be consuming too much text in their diets and getting ill. Too much alphabet soup!

This oral-aural deficiency may be as detrimental physically and mentally to a person as vitamin deficiency, sunlight deficiency, sleep deficiency, or motion deficiency—all evolutionary-based pathologies rooted in human genetics.

Medical science has understood for a while the importance of vitamins in preventing beri-beri, rickets, scurvy, and, more recently, cancer. Now scientists are beginning to research the detrimental effects on our health caused both by the lack of sunlight on our skin and by the failure of our waking-sleeping schedules to line up with our innate, sunlight-determined, circadian biorhythms. No one, however, seems to be researching the detrimental effects of oral-aural deficiency.

In the late 1970s, I worked for three years as a clerk-typist in the OB-GYN clinic of a public hospital in the San Francisco Bay Area. For four hours each day, I would type columns of patients' payment records on an IBM Selectric typewriter in the days before office computers were common. At the end of each day's work, barely able to stand up, I'd stumble around trying to collect my things, eyes glazed, shoulders stiff, neck aching, totally unable to speak coherently to anyone. If a nurse or fellow clerk asked me what my plans were for that evening, I'd just look back at them dry-mouthed, thick-tongued, and silent. I couldn't even mumble an answer.

Scuba divers, while swimming too deep and staying down too long, might experience nitrogen overload, a life-threatening lack of oxygen and over-balance of nitrogen in their bloodstream. Like these divers, I, at the end of each workday, experienced writer's nitrogen overload, a lack of oral-aural oxygen also known (by this writer) as scriptitis. It sometimes took hours of lying sprawled on my "beach"—my living room couch—before the effects wore off.

At least I knew that I was in trouble. Many avid readers don't. Unaware of the danger that awaits them below, they plunge deep into text for hours, days, or weeks at a time. Deprived of orality, they not only experience scriptitis, but their behavior mimics that of some scuba divers caught in the thrall of nitrogen narcosis—the dreaded "rapture of the deep."

"High" from lack of oxygen, scuba divers hit with the "rapture" can start to lose their survival instincts. They've even been known to smilingly remove their air hose from their mouth and offer it to a passing fish. Analogously, avid text-divers, "high" on reading and not wanting to leave their books, can experience "scrivener's rapture of the deep." Smiling all the while, they can be in danger of losing their innate, oral-aural survival instincts, and not even know it or feel it.

Continuing the analogy, scuba divers who swim from the depths to the surface too rapidly, without pausing frequently to decompress, can develop the bends. Deep literates, like ourselves, who might be motivated to quit their texts "cold turkey" and to try to surface too quickly into the new oral culture of the VIVO Age, might find themselves suffering from the Gutenberg bends. By pausing frequently in their ascent in order to study VIVOlutionary skills, they will allow their minds and bodies to decompress slowly from literacy's heavy pressure and to readapt to their natural spoken-word environment.

My work experience at the hospital staring at and creating columns of letters and numbers hour after hour was a numbing experience that gave me a newfound respect, and concern, for people who do this type of work their whole lives. Thousands, perhaps millions, of people in the industrialized countries continue to work these kinds of jobs, laboring at keyboards of one kind or other inputting and reading data day after day after day.

Many workers leave their keyboards at the end of each day as mentally zonked, physically stifled, and orally incapable of social interaction and conversation with others as I was. Others hit the outdoors chattering nonstop, as their bodies and minds try to compensate for the massive, hours-long shutdown of their speech apparatuses. Whatever their symptoms, I worry about them.

Urgent! Reader, please note! If you've read these first four chapters without taking a break, *stop reading now!* Stand up, stretch, and start *talking* to someone.

Musing 2

As we walk the written-language bridge toward oral culture, we seem to be retracing, but in reverse order, the steps our ancestors took to develop written language. We seem to be deconstructing written language in stages that mirror or parallel, but in reverse order, the stages of written language's construction over the last 10,000 years.

If this assumption is true—and I think that it is—then, by understanding those historical steps or stages of written language's construction, we can better understand how we're deconstructing written language now and how we'll continue to deconstruct it through the first half of the 21st Century.

What were those major steps that humanity took to achieve written language? There were three: picture-objects, pictographs-hieroglyphs, and phonetic alphabets.

Step 1 = Picture-Objects

Before they had written language, our ancestors used both memory and picture-objects to store and retrieve information. Picture-objects, such as the ancient drawings we find on cave walls, are really universal (at least, universal within one community) visual symbols and icons. Our ancestors told stories or recorded events using graphics that everyone in the community could interpret and understand.

Though these cave-wall symbols had meaning, they were not written language, not text, not even hieroglyphs. People drew them and interpreted them, but they didn't write or read them. This is because writing and reading are methods for storing and retrieving *language*.

Why didn't the cave-wall drawings constitute a genuine written language? Because they didn't have the combination of elements that turn visual symbols into written language: semantic, syntactic, and phonological rules.

One of today's universal visual symbols is McDonald's golden arches. We don't *read* McDonald's golden arches; we don't even read a picture of the arches. The golden arches, on a building or a billboard, are a picture-object, a visual symbol that stores the message "this is a McDonald's restaurant." We retrieve the message when we see the golden arches and recall its meaning. Then we decide to drive past the place or to pull in for a meal.

Reading and writing is reserved for words, and words are words just because they're units of speech (or signing) that follow specified semantic, syntactic, and phonological rules. When we see the shapes S, T, O, and P, in that order, painted on a red octagonal sign at a traffic intersection in an English-speaking country, we, who are literate in English, assume they're four letters of the English alphabet and assume they're spelling the English word "STOP." Reading involves making these rule-based assumptions.

Someone who was nonliterate, or unfamiliar with the English alphabet and stop signs, would not make those assumptions about the four shapes and, therefore, would not recognize "STOP" as a *word.* They would not recognize it as an example of *writing.* Though they could try to interpret the meaning of the four shapes, they'd be guessing, not *reading.*

Step 2 = Pictographic Words-Hieroglyphs

Some of the Egyptian hieroglyphs started life not as hieroglyphs, but as picture-objects, as universal (among the Egyptians) visual symbols. These symbols became hieroglyphs—pictographic words in a written language—when they were strung together with other hieroglyphic and phonetically-based written words according to a specific set of agreed-upon rules.

Step 3 = Phonetic Alphabets

Visual symbols representing speech sounds became letters when they were combined with other letters to form words, which were combined with other words into sentences, and so on, according to a specific set of agreed-upon rules.

Humanity created written language chronologically by way of Steps 1, 2, and 3. Now, as we in the electronically-developed countries begin to replace written language with speech, we seem to be following a course that is taking us from Step 3, back through Step 2, and on to Step 1.

As the school literacy rate remains stagnant, and people of all ages continue to drop Step 3 alphabet-based written languages in favor of oral-aural methods of accessing stored information, Step 2 pictographic words are beginning to appear more frequently in our written languages, and more Step 1 universal symbols are crowding our visual fields.

Glossaries of Internet pictographs regularly appear in "How to Use the Internet" books. These are providing us with a new vocabulary to help us act upon a felt need: the Step 2-type need to substitute pictographic words for some alphabetic words as we compose our intimate chat-room messages. The semantic and syntactic rules for using ":-)" and ":-(" have already become standardized among Netizens. And let's not forget "@," which adorns all of our email addresses.

I have also noticed a rapid increase in the number of pictographs that my adult students are using in their written notes to me. Perhaps 50% of the handwritten notes I have received from students recently, especially notes with an emotional content—asking me to excuse their absence or asking for more time to complete an assignment—have included a Smiley Face ☺ among their words. "I would appreciate it ☺ if you would...." For some people, ol' Smiley Face is able to express an emotion that they feel might be too risky to express in alphabetic terms.

These new additions to our written languages are our hieroglyphs. They represent not sounds (as letters of the alphabet do), but ideas or themes—the characteristic feature of all pictographic words—yet they combine with alphabetic words and other pictographs to form sentences. When we inject these "Smileys" into our online chats, and these Smiley Faces into our emotional messages, we're introducing Step 2 elements into our written-language word mix.

I think we will see, around 2030, in the electronically-developed countries, a brief period in which neo-hieroglyphs such as "Smiley Face" will take the place of most alphabetical words in the writing of people who are still able to write. In the next few years, look for enterprising computer-hardware manufacturers, following the lead of late-20th Century bumper-sticker makers ("I ❤ New York!"), to begin producing keyboards with many more pictographic keys alongside the alphabetical keys.

We have also surrounded ourselves with hundreds of universally-recognized and/or locally-recognized Step 1 visual symbols and icons: travel and traffic signs, medical symbols, company logos, product logos, Internet and other computer-software icons, spray-painted street-gang tags and other self-identification graffiti. When a McDonald's counterperson takes a Big Mac order by punching a computer key with a picture of a Big Mac on it, they're working on the Step 1 level. The Big Mac key symbol isn't a word, not even a hieroglyphic word; it's a picture-object. And the counterperson isn't reading the key symbol; they're seeing it and interpreting its meaning.

A cave-wall-painting war of sorts is taking place in the United States on that most popular of artistic surfaces: car exteriors. It's the fish versus the fish-with-feet. Translation: some cars display a chrome fish, symbolizing the driver's belief in Jesus Christ and, perhaps by extension, the account of the universe's creation as literally stated in the *Bible's* Book of Genesis. Other cars sport a fish-with-feet, signaling the driver's rejection of Genesis and their acceptance of Darwinism and evolution.

By mid-21st Century, as we step off the written-language bridge into an environment overflowing with Step 1 visual symbols, we will have already abandoned both our Step 3 alphabetical texts and our Step 2 hieroglyphic texts. In their place, we will have re-embraced the twin pillars of oral-aural information storage and retrieval—not in the form of the human-brain memory and human-constructed picture-objects of 10,000 years ago, but in the form of their respective 2050 reincarnations: VIVO memory and VIVO graphics.

Let's take one last dive into the Twilight Zone to finish out this chapter. A principle of evolutionary biology says that "ontogeny recapitulates phylogeny." It means that each animal life form on Earth passes through embryonic-fetal-infantile stages of development that mirror the development of all animal life forms that, evolutionarily, preceded it.

Simply stated, it means, for example, that a human embryo will begin life resembling the first class of living creatures on Earth—a one-celled animal—and will then develop through fetal stages in which it more or less resembles, respectively, a fish, an amphibian, a reptile, a non-human mammal, and finally a human mammal.

Can we apply a similar analogous principle to the evolutionary pathway each person follows in acquiring literacy skills—and to the pathway they'll follow as they lose those skills? This application of "ontogeny recapitulates phylogeny" would say that a nonliterate child or adult develops writing skills in stages that reflect the historical stages of written language's development. It would go on to say that a literate person will lose writing skills, in the 21st Century, in stages that reflect the historical stages of written language's demise.

In this Musing, I've already presented what I believe are the historical stages of written language's development (Steps 1, 2, 3) and future demise (Steps 3, 2, 1). The "recapitulation" principle now becomes a useful tool for analyzing the stages of development and/or loss of an individual person's writing skills.

We give 5-year-old Yan-Rong, who's learning to read and write, a pencil and paper and ask her to write something. We can establish the stage of her writing skills by looking at what she does.

Is she mostly drawing picture-objects? **[♀/人]**

Mostly writing pictographic-hieroglyphic words? **[I ♥ ♀/人]**

Or mostly writing alphabetic words? **[I LOVE MOMMY]**

Once we can establish her writing-skills stage, we can develop teaching techniques specifically designed to help Yan-Rong reach the next stage.

What about Kathy, the mid-21st Century protagonist of this book's Prologue, who learned to read and write by joining an extracurricular Written Language Club when she was ten and then, over the next 25 years, lost her literacy skills through disuse, thanks to talking computers? By applying the "recapitulation" principle to her case, we can presume that her writing loss followed a trajectory from mostly writing alphabetic words, to mostly writing pictographic words, to finally replacing all writing with speech and picture-objects/universal symbols in conjunction with her VIVO-computer's speech and graphics functions.

As more of us literati in the electronically-developed countries begin to emulate Kathy, forgetting how to write and replacing our writing skills with compspeak, we'll want to be able to gauge just how far each of us has progressed toward oracy. Just as we now test the rates at which students are learning how to write, we'll soon want to also test the rates at which people are *forgetting* how to write. By testing the writing and determining the precise writing-skills stage of someone who is losing their writing skills, we'll be better able to help that person acquire the VIVOlutionary-learning skills that will enable them to function more successfully in their new oral-culture home.

PART II

Recreating an
Oral Culture

VIVOlutionary Learning: Next Step in Re/Storing Education and Human Consciousness

hen the retina in one of my eyes detached years ago, I faced a major re-attachment operation followed by two weeks on my back in bed with patches over both eyes. To keep me mentally active, a friend went out and got me, from the city's library for people with visual disabilities, a variable-speed audiocassette player and a few spoken-book audiocassettes of novels.

It took me 30 seconds, from the moment I inserted my first cassette and started to listen, to realize that I was totally unprepared for this new experience. I was hit with several problems all at once.

1. The words of the story were going by too quickly to comprehend what was being said, nor was there enough time to remember what had previously been said in order to join it together with what was now being said. 2. My attention span was

too short to follow the drift of the story for more than a minute or two. With nothing to focus on visually (like print), I couldn't keep my mind on what was being said. 3. I kept trying to picture what the words would look like written out on the page, and this pulled my attention away from the verbal flow of words. 4. The voice of the reader, a male with an unpleasant nasal tone and strong Boston accent, was distracting, and I found myself spending time trying to picture what he looked like. 5. The cassette was probably old and definitely much-used; its popping, crackling, and hissing masked some of the words and created an overall distracting ambiance. 6. I wasn't familiar enough with the cassette player's controls, so my initial efforts to slow the speed and adjust the tone and volume, while continuing to follow the story, were failures. With much fumbling, I was finally able to turn the damn thing off and take a deep breath.

Improving my use of the system took patient (and sometimes impatient) experimentation. One thing that helped immensely was to get myself thinking and believing that I was listening to someone speaking over the radio rather than to someone reading a book aloud. As long as I took the voice to be reading a book, which is how I first approached the situation, all of my print-oriented, book-reading experience and skills demanded to be called into play.

Shepherded along by my bookish mindset, I wanted to see the words on the page. I wanted to control the speed at which the words went by—sometimes faster, sometimes slower, as I do when I read—in order to allow my imagination to work at its desired pace with regard to the content. I wanted to go back and reprocess groups of words to better comprehend their meaning and/or to appreciate their selection by the author. I wanted to get rid of those aural distractions—that unpleasant nasal voice, those pops and hisses—and substitute the soft, even sound of my own breathing, the sound I hear when I read.

The more I could convince myself that the voice was that of someone speaking to me over the radio instead of reading aloud to me, the better I could assimilate the elements of this experience. If there was one thing I knew, it was radio voices.

As a child, in the years before TV had entered my home, I had gotten hooked on radio. I'd rush home from school with my friends, and we'd lie on a bed and listen to the adventures of Jack Armstrong the All-American Boy, Tennessee Jed, the Lone Ranger, Sergeant Preston of the Yukon, Sky King, and Bobby Benson and the B-Bar-B Ranch. Later in the evening, after I'd gone to bed, I'd listen to The Shadow, Boston Blackie, and The Green Hornet.

Like most young people of my generation, I had developed significant listening skills, thanks to the radio. (The fact that Boston Blackie and the rest were reading their lines from written scripts was irrelevant to my aural experience.) I could process those audio narratives as fast as they were fed to me, topped with all the pops and hisses my cheapo radio's signal could produce. Believe me, I didn't miss a word or a nuance of meaning. When it came time to write down the address of an advertiser to whom I'd send my fifty cents and two cereal boxtops for some gizmo, I'd only have to hear it once to remember it perfectly.

We were the last radio generation. From the moment, each afternoon, that the final bell sent us racing out of the schoolyard toward home, we kids constituted our own radio-driven oral culture. With the coming of the TV age, I and my peers lost those specialized listening and aural-imagining abilities that we had honed through our countless hours in the company of Jack Armstrong and Tennessee Jed.

Fortunately, as I was recovering from eye surgery, I was able to reach back to that early radio-listening experience and use it to alter and improve my responses to my subsequent spoken-book experiences. Once I said to myself (though I knew I was fooling myself), "Hey, it (the spoken-book) isn't a book, it's a radio show!" my mind's insistence on using my book-reading skills diminished, I relaxed and let the vocal (and other) sounds flow in, and my comprehension and enjoyment of the spoken-book novels soared.

Soon I was operating the variable speed lever on the audio-cassette player like an automobile gearshift stick, shifting down when I hit a stretch of words that I wanted to go by slower, and shifting up when I wanted them to zoom by. As the days went by, I found myself shifting up higher and higher; I couldn't stand to listen to the narrator's voice unless it sounded like Alvin the Chipmunk's voice flying through the text at top speed.

What lessons did I learn from this traumatic adventure with a happy ending? One lesson was that, when I hit the "play" button of my variable-speed audiocassette player for the first time, I was *out of my element*. I lacked the skills, the know-how, and the perceptual and conceptual equipment and imagination to extract its value.

Another lesson was that, with some practice, I was able to acquire new skills and know-how and reorient my perceptions, conceptions, and imagination to adapt to the audiocassette player. I was able to integrate myself *back into my element*, and, in the process, transform the audiocassette player from an alien object into a piece of my element's furniture. Actually, it was a two-way street: I also became a piece of the audiocassette player's furniture and made the audiocassette player adapt to me.

Daily practice with the audiocassette player had caused my

sense organs-to-brain pathways to (temporarily, at least) re-route or reconfigure themselves from print-visual to oral-aural. It is a shift that everyone who has learned to read and write will have to undergo when they first begin to use talking computers—an initiation or rite of passage into oral culture.

This whole episode was a perfect example of VIVOlutionary learning: through practice I was able to reformat my neural pathways to fit the new oral-aural environment, I improved my listening skills, increased my knowledge of how my mind and senses worked, even improved my cursing...er, speaking...skills.

For those few memorable days after I had perfected my audiocassette-player techniques, I actually experienced life inside an oral culture—not, as anthropologists do, by visiting and studying an oral culture, but by creating my own.

Fortunately or unfortunately—I haven't decided which—my visit to my self-created oral culture was short-lived. Once my eye patches were removed and I began to read and write again, the oral-aural skills I had acquired over the two weeks quickly slipped away. A week after regaining my sight, I had reconfigured my neural pathways back to text-visual.

But I had scaled the oral-aural mountain and reached the summit. I had seen (heard?) it up close. I now know that, with practice, it's possible for a written-language veteran, like myself, to develop the new skills that will allow him or her to enter the VIVO-dominated oral culture of the 21st Century.

The task ahead is twofold: first, to identify the individual skills that we'll need in order to participate fully and effectively in oral culture and, second, to design a training program so that we and others can systematically develop these skills. What follows is my attempt to briefly engage the first of these; the second is a task for another time, another book.

We've begun the transition from text-based to speech-based oral-aural information storage and retrieval, but no one is preparing us, training us, giving our mouths, ears, eyes, and brains the particular kinds of practice they're going to need to store and retrieve information in the VIVO Age. No one is preparing us for the rite of passage looming ahead. Without these skills, we'll be out of our element and without a clue.

From the time we're born—and probably even before, in the womb—we're being initiated into the speech-based method of communicating. People who later become literate shift constantly between speech-based (that is, memory-based) and text-based methods of storing and retrieving information. Like bilingual speakers, literate people are bi-informational, at home in two worlds (add the picture-object non-text-visual world, and it makes three) of freezing and thawing information.

But our schools have focused solely on developing young people uni-informationally. The schools have worked, though not very successfully, to develop young people's writing and reading capabilities, while ignoring their speaking and listening capabilities. This approach perhaps made some sense in the Literacy Age, but, now that we're entering the Post-Literacy Age, it makes no sense at all. People are going to have to acquire new skills to manage information transfer using talking computers, and our education system needs to begin to boot up this process—soon!

In order to effectively access stored information in the 21st Century, people will need to develop these eight, currently-neglected, oral-cultural skills:
1. speaking skills;
2. listening skills;
3. visual skills;
4. time-sound and distance-sound correlation skills;

5. otographic and photographic memory skills;
6. critical thinking skills;
7. creative thinking skills;
8. mathematics without written numerals skills.

1 and 2: Where are the grade-school speaking courses and listening courses that will help young people develop their abilities to store and retrieve VIVO-computer information in the 21st Century? Where are the courses that will help students say precisely what they're thinking in order to input VIVO computers more accurately? Where are the listening courses that students will need to process VIVO-computer output more accurately?

While the great majority of people in the electronically-developed countries do transfer a lot of information by speaking rather than through written language, many are quite inept at expressing their thoughts and feelings verbally. Recordings of people's ordinary conversations often contain little substantive content, little real information. So much of what people intend to convey they often express non-verbally, through facial expressions, hand gestures, other body language, expressive sounds, intonation, pauses, and so on.

In fact, such recordings often contain very few complete sentences, clauses, or even phrases. Vocabulary range is frequently limited to the same several dozen words used over and over throughout the day. Some people's spoken lexicons contain no more than 75 or 100 *different* vocabulary words overall. Talking computers, even more than the telephone, are going to challenge the verbally-challenged. Right?

Well…yes and no. In the not-too-distant future, our VIVOs will have electronic eyes that will be able to scan and incorporate our hand gestures, eyebrow raises, and intonations along with our spoken words as integral parts of our communications. VIVOs will understand the meanings of our uh-huh's, pauses, shrill voices, pursed lips, and smiling faces just as we understand one another's. It follows, then, that in a couple of decades or less, as with telephone use today, some people will interact with their VIVOs using greater numbers of words and more complex usages, while others will stick to smaller lexicons, simpler verbalizations, and a whole lot of gestures.

The latter method may work for casual information accessing, but for more formal, ambitious, and structured storage-retrieval work using talking computers, more sophisticated speaking skills will be required. Can you imagine cranking up your VIVO for a serious, extended educational, scientific, medical, political, commercial, or storytelling conversation using a 75-word vocabulary and a lot of hand waving?

Then there is the matter of speed. Research has shown that, even today, most people can easily speak at rates of 200-300 words per minute (WPM) and can hear and understand speech at rates as high as 500 WPM (from the *Discovering The Human Language* video series, by Gene Searchinger). Where are the speed-speaking and speed-listening courses—parallelling, respectively, shorthand/speed-typing and speed-reading courses—that will allow students to maximize their rates so that they may input VIVO data and comprehend VIVO output faster and more efficiently?

Qualitative listening, however, involves much more than achieving a high hearing-understanding rate. We'll need to be able to let our minds range backward and forward through VIVO's stream of spoken information—as we continue listening to and absorbing the stream.

It's a matter of developing *aurally-ambidextrous minds* that can continue to hear and understand the flow of new spoken information while simultaneously remembering, accessing, searching through, thinking critically and creatively about, reflecting on, and daydreaming about that part of the flow that has already entered our ears. Development of an aurally-ambidextrous mind is linked to skills #4 and #5 below—development of time-sound and distance-sound correlations and an otographic memory.

3: Where are the visual-skills courses that will allow us to "read" or interpret the computer-monitor visuals that will frequently accompany VIVO's aural output? Where's the instruction that will help us update our ancient ability to retrieve information via the picture-object method?

Are we going to be able to "read" the 21st Century equivalent of cave wall paintings? Are we going to be able to understand the tree markings, the broken blades of grass, and the footprints along the electronic trails we'll navigate on our monitors and virtual reality headsets? Our eyes need to be trained to notice and interpret correctly all the visual data that will appear on our wrist-VIVOs' screens or in the computer-generated holograms that will float before our eyes.

Acting on a felt need, young children are already, and for the most part unconsciously, teaching themselves how to do this. Research has shown that when young children watch TV, their eyes continuously and rapidly shift their focus from one part of the screen's image to another. Where the children focus their eyes and attention, however, frequently has little to do with where the so-called "main action" is ostensibly happening.

The children often seem to be more interested in looking at something that's "off in the corner" of the screen than they are in focusing on that part of the TV image that the producer, the director, the sponsor, and most adults would deem most important.

Do these children know something about locating visual information in the Electronic Age that the rest of us don't? They'd better, because they're the ones who are going to have to design the new 21st Century visual-skills courses—and the TV shows.

4: Where are the courses that teach time-sound and distance-sound correlation skills—skills that will assist us in searching orally-aurally and visually for stored information on our talking computers. Time-sound correlation skills allow us to estimate mentally how many seconds or minutes ago our VIVO said something that we want to reaccess. Distance-sound correlation skills allow us to use visual aids such as scroller bars to estimate the location of spoken information we wish to find or reaccess. Chapter 6, "Just Thinking Out Loud: Searching for Information Using Sound and Image but No Text," investigates this further.

5: Where are the memory courses that, by improving students' memory-retention skills, will allow students to hold aural and visual data in their minds for short periods of time and recall it when they need it as they work with their VIVOs? The students' objective will be to develop memories that can retain aural information (= otographic memory; "oto" is the medical prefix meaning "ear") and visual information (= photographic memory) over the short term. Retaining oral-aural and visual information over the long term will be their VIVOs' task.

6 and 7: I think it's urgent to add: where are the critical and creative thinking courses—needed by writers-readers today as well as speakers-listeners today and tomorrow—that we desperately need in order to develop analytical, dialectical, creative, and other types of thinking? How else will we learn to ask the questions and find the answers that will help us solve the world's problems great and small?

8: Finally, where are the courses that we'll need to help us do spoken mathematics, given that our current numeral notational system for representing numbers will soon become obsolete? That's right, we won't be writing or reading numerals because we won't have to. Our VIVOs will become our calculators, and all freezing and thawing of applied-mathematical information, all input and output relating to non-theoretical calculations and figuring, will take place orally-aurally—much of this also in tandem with computer-generated visual aids. Chapter Seven, "Written Numerals, Your Number's Up! And VIVO's Got Your Number!" continues this discussion.

Almost always, when I speak to groups about these VIVOlutionary learning skills, the discussion evokes the following questions from the audience. *Who* will we *be* in the VIVO Age? What will people be like? Will our great-great grandchildren living in their oral cultures be fundamentally different than we, their print-literate forebears? Will their consciousness and their thinking be similar to ours? Will they perceive and conceive the world, reality, as we do? If they truly won't be able to read and write, as *VIVO [Voice-In/Voice-Out]* forecasts, will they still be able to really think—especially to think logically and scientifically? And will they still retain our incredible ability to gather information visually—an ability we've developed and exercise everyday through reading and writing?

These are large, important questions deserving of deeper consideration than I can give here. For the remainder of this chapter, I'll sketch some responses to these questions that might suggest directions for further thought and study. First, let's look at the question of whether people born into a VIVO Age oral culture will be able to think logically and scientifically.

There is a popularly held belief that only through learning to read and write can an individual, or a whole society, begin to think logically and scientifically. Literacy, according to this view, is a necessary prerequisite for logical thought. This belief rests on the assumption that one's learning to read and write, and only this activity, formats a part of one's brain—or, alternatively, unlocks an already formatted part of one's brain—in a way that allows one's brain to think linearly-logically.

The argument goes something like this. Written language is linear and sequential. As we view and absorb such word-follows-word and sentence-follows-sentence sequences, our thinking also becomes linear and sequential. Sequential thought opens the door to logical thought, which, in turn, opens the door to scientific and mathematical thought, and even to moral thought. Literacy, and only literacy, can trigger or create these thought patterns.

Reading, writing, logical reasoning, modern science, and morality are a package deal, says this view. Lose reading and writing, and the rest will go, too. As proof, it points to past and present oral cultures, where, it declares, the lack of reading and writing goes hand-in-hand with the lack of "civilization" itself.

This is serious business, according to this view, because the so-called "uncivilized" nonliterates who will be populating our 21st Century electronically-developed countries in the VIVO Age will be—like Mary Beth and Thomas in this book's Prologue—our own great-great grandchildren.

Unable to formulate linearly-based, logically-based distinctions such as I-other and cause-effect, our oral-aural progeny will live their lives as mental "primitives," trapped inside their syncretic-oceanic-subjective mode of thought, and lacking any true sense of individual self-identity, personhood, and personal responsibility.

If talking computers, like a contemporary Pied Piper, do lead us into a worldwide oral culture, this view concludes, the electronically-developed nations will be thrown headlong into a 21st Century Stone Age, benighted, living in ignorance, chaos, and moral turpitude. A true Doomsday scenario.

I see things differently. First, on what basis does this Doomsday view select out—from the vast realm of our sense experiences—our visualization of textual sequences as the only experiences that can lead us to linear-sequential thought? If the assumption that sequential experiences can trigger or create sequential thought patterns is true, then all sorts of sequential experiences should be able to do the job, not just our visual exposure to text.

We, both literates and nonliterates, are surrounded by and experience innumerable other visual, auditory, tactile, olfactory, and gustatory sequences in our daily lives. Why can't these also lead to linear-sequential thought? Have the Doomsdayers, carrying their pro-text bias with them, already prejudged the winner here before walking into the arena?

Speech, the characteristic mark of an oral culture, is itself sequential and uni-directional. Couldn't our exposure to the word-follows-word sequences of spoken language also encourage logical thought? Then, there are all the other sequences that form the basic experience of both oral-aural and print-literate people: the rising and setting of the sun and moon, the seasonal cycle, the regular movement of stars across the sky, the life cycle itself: birth-growth-aging-death, our mode of walking step-by-step-by-step.

People in oral cultures, like print-literate people, recognize and utilize causal relationships between events. They use medicines to cure disease, tools to gather needed substances and to build needed objects, dialogue to avoid conflict. Education, commerce and trade, government, healing, food production and gathering, science, engineering, mathematics, ritual, art, celebration, law, morality, and spirituality/religion are integral to their lives. All of these life-sustaining activities require the types of thought that Western societies call induction and deduction. Who says that individuals and societies need written language to think logically!

Finally, it was none other than our *nonliterate*, oral-culture ancestors who created the Doomsdayers' very paradigm of linearity and sequentiality: written language itself. Could they have done that if they hadn't already been able to think linearly and sequentially?

Conversely, just as nonliterate people can—and do—think sequentially and logically, literate people can—and do—think nonsequentially and nonlogically. Through our daydreams and asleep dreams, our imaginings, our irrational fears and hopes, our intuitions and inspirations, our faith-based spiritual beliefs, our beliefs in chance, contingency, and even free will, we print-literates daily perceive and conceive our world nonlinearly, as well as linearly.

In a word, *all* human beings, whether literate or nonliterate, actively engage in *both* sequential and nonsequential perception and thought. Without *both* modes, survival would be impossible. Though our post-literate great-great grandchildren won't write or read, they—like everyone before them and everyone after them—will also think both logically and nonlogically.

Taking it a step further, I predict that our oral-aural great-great-grandchildren in the VIVO-driven societies of 2050 and beyond will be even more highly expert at linear-logical modes of thought than we are today. Check out the following article headlined "Spelling Skills Decline in Germany."

"Young Germans are losing the ability to spell, despite the

language's relative consistency and close correspondence to pro-nunciation. Professors at the University of Heidelberg tested 600 native speakers aged 16 to 30 on their ability to correctly transcribe dictated text. Nearly 40 percent received grades of 'inadequate,' compared with 5 percent in a 1968 study.

"Declining spelling skills may be the result of a decline in reading and increased exposure to nonwritten forms of com-munication such as graphics-heavy computers, the researchers speculate. Today's German youth *score higher on intelligence tests* than did their counterparts in 1977, and they *do markedly better in comprehending visually presented information.*" (My italics— from *The Week in Germany*, April 17, 1998; reprinted in *The Futurist*, November, 1998.)

The fact that these young Germans scored higher on intel-ligence tests—tests that require analytical and logical skills— even as their writing skills declined underscores my point. Nonliteracy and logical thinking are compatible.

Another valuable lesson drawn from these tests is that the youths' visual comprehension increased despite their decreasing literacy skills. This provides a nice segue to a second frequently-asked question regarding how our VIVO Age descendants will perceive reality. Won't we become *less visual* in an oral culture? By emphasizing VIVOlutionary learning skills and de-emphasizing literacy skills, won't our eyes get smaller as our ears get bigger?

The answer is no. We'll actually improve our ability to gather information with our eyes, and with our other sense organs as well. In fact, we print-literates are *not* very visual compared to people who live in oral cultures. Our visuality is trained to recognize written language, period. Not only doesn't our text-recognition ability carry over to other, non-text visual situations, but they seem to work in inverse proportion to each other: the better we are at gathering textual information, the worse we are at gathering visual information in non-text situations, and vice versa.

Try it yourself. Look up at the ceiling, and without looking down, describe the pattern on the carpet under your feet. See, we're not nearly as visual as we think we are. When we compare our visual information-gathering skill with that of people in oral cultures who have to rely more heavily than we on *all* of their sense organs for information gathering and processing, it's no contest.

Oral culturians continuously focus all of their senses and sense organs simultaneously on a dynamic, changing reality. Never do they do that which we textualites do every time we read or write: separate out one sense (such as visuality) from the others and focus that sense on a static reality (such as text).

For a person living in an oral culture, gathering and processing information means having all sense organs working in harmony and in concert, improvising together moment by moment, and playing at their peak performance level—the sensory system as a swinging jazz combo.

I believe that all humans, barring disabilities, are born with this intensely interactive mode of sense perception, along with the potential to produce correlated thought patterns. Growing up in an oral culture nurtures these "jazzy" sensory systems, while learning to read and write replaces our jazz combo with a solo musician (our eyes) able only to read the notes on the sheet music (text) and not much else.

The Doomsdayers and other thinkers have mistakenly labeled this innate sensory-thought system as a "subjective" mindset, and have mistakenly argued that it is incapable of linear-logical thought. They're wrong. Our innate mentalities are not "subjective"; they're "just" *fully* operational. They may *appear*, from the shrunken perspective of *print-literate* researchers, to generate only nonlinear and illogical perceptions and thoughts, but, as we know, appearances can deceive.

This heightened unity of sensory experience in the act of gathering and processing information stands at the root of our notion of "*common sense.*" *The Oxford English Dictionary (O.E.D.)* (Second Edition, Volume III, Clarendon Press, Oxford, p. 573), citing Greek and Latin roots, begins its first definition of "common sense" this way: "An 'internal' sense which was regarded as the common bond or centre of the five senses, in which the various impressions received were reduced to the unity of a common consciousness."

As Aristotle, the ancient Greek philosopher, put it (according to Sir William Hamilton in *Reid's Works*, 1842, cited by the *O.E.D.*, page 573), "common sense" is "the faculty in which the various reports of the several senses are reduced to the unity of a common apperception."

In the same vein, Robert Burton, (in *Anatomy of Melancholy*, 1621, cited by the *O.E.D.*, page 573) writes: "Inner senses are three in number, so called, because they be within the brainpan, as Common Sense, Phantasie, Memory. This Common sense is the Judge or Moderator of the rest, by whom we discern all differences of objects…. The external senses and the common sense considered together are like a circle with five lines drawn from the circumference to the centre."

The *O.E.D.*'s second definition of "common sense" is the meaning that we tend to think of today when we use the term: "The endowment of natural intelligence possessed by rational beings; ordinary, normal or average understanding; the plain wisdom which is everyone's inheritance." (p. 573)

It's important, I think, to see how the second, more modern

of these two definitions flows from, and is based on, the first, more ancient one. What we think of as "common sense" today—the "natural intelligence" and "plain wisdom" which is "everyone's inheritance"—is rooted in the idea of "common sense" as "the unity of a common consciousness" or "common apperception." In ordinary language, this means that ordinary common sense/natural intelligence requires that our senses be always intertwined and working together when processing information.

Looking at things this way, only people who operate with all of their sense organs working in unison, collectively—that is, *networking*—can possess common sense. And who are they? The oral culturians, for whom the practice of VIVOlutionary learning skills is a way of life 24 hours a day.

Many of today's artists, though literate, are also able to model this oral-culturian consciousness. As they create visual arts, music, or dance, they temporarily suspend/transcend their textualite consciousnesses, reformatting them into swinging neural networks that can perceive and guide their emerging art works.

The lesson here for us, as we move toward oral culture, is that developing VIVOlutionary learning skills and developing a unified consciousness are inextricably linked. Any progress we make in acquiring, improving, and using VIVOlutionary skills will spur the re-integration and re-networking of our neural-sensory system. And the more unified our consciousness becomes, the better we'll be able to use our VIVOlutionary skills. It's a mutual-aid process—a two-way causal street.

Who, then, will we *be* in 2050's oral culture? Depending on the course of events over the next five decades, and factoring in a good stiff dose of VIVOlutionary learning, we—or, more precisely, our great-great grandchildren—will most likely be people who will have more unified consciousnesses and greatly heightened sense perceptions, who will think both logically and nonlogically, and who will possess a lot more common sense than we do today.

While the possibility of creating *artificial* intelligence remains a juicy topic of debate in information-technology circles, we actually create artificial intelligence every time we begin to teach a child or adult to write and read. By fracturing the innate unity of human perception and thought, of consciousness itself, literacy training reformats our minds, creating in us a non-natural, artificial intelligence.

In fact, by reconfiguring the "unified fields" of our minds into "non-unified fields," literacy negatively affects our ability to access, view, and understand the real world in a consistently unified and intelligent way. Might this be why the literate scientific establishment has been unable so far to develop a sound, experimentally provable unified-field theory of the universe?

Lastly, VIVOs will soon be recognized as the true time machines. Sci-fi offers a vision of time machines that transport us, with our present mindsets, into a past or future society. No, the true time machine is a technology that changes and heals our presently-fractured, text-literate human consciousness so that we become, mentally at least, like oral culturians of the past, present, and future. VIVOs will take us "back to the future" without our ever leaving home.

Earlier in this chapter, I said that no one is preparing us for the kinds of oral-aural experiences we'll face and the VIVOlutionary learning skills we'll need as we attempt to master 21st Century VIVO technology. I take that back. Rap groups and some kinds of rock groups—punk, heavy metal—have been effectively training young people in Listening 101 via stereo, radio, TV, Internet, and CD-ROM. Faced with having to translate and repeat often difficult-to-understand raps and lyrics that are usually accompanied by loud drumbeats, young people pass the test every time.

Maybe the first generation of VIVO users will have to accompany their VIVOs' voice-outs with booming *drumbeat* samples. It will be their way of reaching back to their rap-and-rock-listening experience and using it to help them *hear* what their VIVOs are saying—just as I reached back to my radio-listening experience to help me hear what my variable-speed audiocassette player was saying.

CHAPTER 6

Just Thinking Out Loud: Searching for Information Using Sound and Image but No Text

"That's ridiculous! Our eyes can scan text on our computer monitors—or anywhere—*much* faster than we can listen to the same words being spoken. Our sense of sight is *much* more developed than our sense of hearing. Plus, when we read, we can scan backwards and forwards, up and down the page or screen, but when we listen, we have to accept the sounds in the order they're presented to us. Reading gives us a flexibility that's missing when we just listen.

"Plus, when we're searching text for information by computer and aren't exactly sure what's out there or available, we're able to use search engines to reach lists of relevant topics, quickly eyeball their content, and access only the items we need. No way we'd be able to do this as easily by listening to our computers talk.

"Imagine trying to search through long lists of data by ear, rather than by eye. It would take forever. We'd have to listen to the whole list just to find out if there's any item on the list that we'd want to access.

"Plus, storing speech requires so much more memory than storing text does. Who has the money to pay for all that memory? Not me. There's no way that voice-driven computers are going to totally replace text-driven computers by 2050—or ever. The thesis of your book is all wrong."

Pretty devastating critique, huh? Then why are computer companies, governments, and university computer-science departments putting out big bucks and charging ahead full blast to research and develop talking computers? Do they know something that the naysayers don't?

Let's break down the critique into its separate points and reply to each.

Critique point #1: Searching for information using text and eye is more efficient than searching for it orally-aurally using voice and ear.

The advantage of text, according to the critique, is that we can quickly read indexes and data and choose which items we want to access by clicking on them. This becomes very effective using hypertext—boldfaced keywords—to direct us to our areas of interest. Suppose we don't exactly know what we're looking for, and we just want to scan lists of data hoping to spot a juicy item that might point our inquiry in a helpful direction. Wouldn't reading the available data off a display monitor be more efficient than conversing with a VIVO?

One problem, the critique continues, with using speech to seek and receive information is that spoken language is temporal. One spoken word follows another; one spoken sentence follows another. It takes too much precious time to speak to a talking computer, and too much precious time to hear what it has to say back to us.

With a screen full of text, we're not limited by having to listen to a uni-directional spoken-word stream. The eyes of highly-literate readers can actively skim and locate information with a flexibility and efficiency unmatched by their ears—ears which must wait passively, forever at the mercy of the one-sentence-after-another aural flow.

Reply to point #1: Imagine that we lived in an *oral-aural* culture and had just invented talking computers. How would we want to interact with our VIVOs when using them to search for information? Our first choice would be to use the models and methods we've employed in our daily conversations with other people. We'd want to talk to our VIVOs the way we talked to other people, and we'd want them to talk to us the same way.

Think about how we talk to each other when we're searching for information in our ordinary conversations. I ask, "Sally, where's the best place to buy a swimsuit?" Sally doesn't normally answer with a long list of every place that I can buy a swimsuit. She asks me questions:

Sally: "What price?"

I: "About fifteen or twenty dollars."

Sally: "What style?"

I: "I'm not sure. I want to look at different styles and try some on."

Sally: "So you want to go to a store instead of shopping online?"

I: "Yes."

Sally: "How far are you willing to travel?"

I: "Not more than fifteen miles total."

Sally: "What hours are you available to go shopping?"

I: "I work until 5:30 p.m., so it'll have to be some place

that's open evenings."

Sally: "I suggest you go to Duncan's at Outlet Mall."

Let's call this common, everyday way of verbally searching for and accessing information "thinking out loud" (TOL). VIVOs will be programmed to think out loud like Sally did. I'll talk to my VIVO just like I talked to Sally.

This conversational search method actually resembles the method we print-literates use all the time to search for information on the Internet and World Wide Web. I started my search by giving Sally—my human "search engine"—keywords and/or words denoting general categories: "best place," "buy," "swimsuit." Sally's questioning opened up more specific categories, and, together, we finally arrived at the answer I wanted. Think oral-aural equivalents of hypertext.

The assumption that my VIVO will be forever bombarding me with an endless cacophony of spoken sentences, each sentence of which I will have to patiently listen to in the order it's presented to me and then choose to either select or bypass, is unfounded. The assumption itself reflects the stranglehold on our (literate) thought processes exerted by the linearity of text.

If I want to find out from you what hippopotamuses eat for breakfast, I don't usually ask you my question and then listen patiently while you relate every known fact in the world about hippos until you happen to mention their breakfast choices. No, I just ask you, "What do hippos eat for breakfast?" and you tell me.

The "Sally" and "hippo" examples provide the solution to Critique #1's concern that communicating with VIVOs will require listening to encyclopedia-length selections of spoken "paragraphs" and huge "lists" of spoken data—analogous to the written paragraphs and indexes that appear on our computer monitors today. It's an important point, since this assumption, that we *will* have to listen to all that verbal detritus in order to find anything, underlies much of the skepticism about VIVO's usefulness as a future storer and retriever of information. The assumption, however, is unwarranted and false.

Rest assured, we *won't* be spending the VIVO Age wallowing like hippos in an interminable river of unwanted speech. We simply aren't going to have to deal with those spoken "paragraphs" and long "lists." Critique #1's assumption, that we will have to, is wrong because it, itself, is based on a *textual model.* It comes from our experience of searching *textual* sources for information and of using our *text-driven* computers as our search tools.

But that model doesn't work for talking computers. We have got to drop all text-based models when we think about searching for information using VIVOs. We will not be spending our lives doing all that tedious and unnecessary listening. That's not the way VIVOs will work.

When we interact with talking computers, we will use *thinking principles* to search for new information and to reaccess old information. By using thinking principles, I mean we'll mentally leap from concept to concept, and idea to idea, using mind compasses based on such categories of critical and creative thought as comparison, contrast, analogy, metaphor, subjective symbolism, cause and effect, general-to-specific, specific-to-general, and so on.

When we ask our VIVOs about hippo breakfasts, we and our VIVOs won't be exchanging *every possible* bit of hippo information, because that's not the way we think—and that's not the way we'll program our VIVOs to think. Just as Sally and I did in the swimsuit example, we and our talking computers will ask each other questions, answer them, ask further questions, correct each other's errors, make constructive suggestions—all part of the process of our locating the information we're searching for.

In a nutshell, we'll *converse* with our VIVOs. That's why I call our future interactions with VIVOs "thinking out loud"— because conversing *is* thinking out loud. It's a knack most people have already acquired—although most of us literates will probably need to sharpen our TOL skills with a course or two in VIVOlutionary-learning techniques.

What *do* hippos eat for breakfast?

Critique point #2: Our eyes are quicker than our ears, and can take in more; we can read more information more quickly than we can hear it. Human biology—that's why talking computers will never replace text-driven computers.

Reply to #2: VIVO users in the 21st Century will have acquired a knapsack full of improved oral-aural skills for interacting with their computers. Most literate people today, though we possess some of these skills, qualify as bottom-rung, oral-aural amateurs. Our great-grandchildren will be able to speak and listen at significantly higher rates and in qualitatively new ways.

For this reason, I just don't buy the argument that talking computers will be impractical because we can't scan oral-aural output as fast as we can scan textual output. In a few years, we'll be able to speak and hear at rates thought impossible today— when we'll need to. Most of the time, however, we'll be accessing our VIVOs' stored information by talking at normal conversational rates, as I did when I spoke with Sally about swimsuits.

We will develop new speed-speaking and speed-listening skills for accessing our VIVOs, but we'll use them only on special occasions—just as we do today when we converse with people. There are those infrequent times when we have to talk faster—and listen faster—and we're able to do it.

How many of us, to save time or out of impatience, occasionally hold down the "fast forward" button on our telephone answering machines while listening to our messages? Our answering machines are already helping us to improve our speed-listening skills despite our love-hate relationship with these gadgets. (Very soon, we'll be showing our gratitude to our answering machines by tossing them into the trash along with our telephones, computers, and TVs in favor of a new, wireless, Internet-based family of appliances that performs all these functions.)

In addition, our conversations with our VIVOs won't have to be in the form of complete, grammatically-correct sentences. Each of us will speak as we normally speak and will program our VIVOs to speak as we speak. Not only our own VIVOs, but *all* VIVOs will speak to each of us in our own variant(s) of our own spoken language(s) or, if we wish, in any other variant(s), vocal style(s), and language(s) we select.

Whenever I log on, I will be electronically informing any VIVO that I want it to speak to me according to my precoded instructions—or according to new instructions that I am encoding it with. Since any VIVO that I use to access information will speak as I wish it to, I'll be able to comprehend it easily and efficiently.

To increase a VIVO's user-friendliness, I could even program it to utter those other sounds—I hesitate to call them "nonwords" since they probably *are* words—we make when we speak: the ones that have clear meanings when spoken but not when transcribed onto the page: uh huh, uh uh, uh oh, mmm hmm.

VIVOs will also have a seeing-eye capability, which will allow them to read our facial expressions and body language, as well as a hearing-ear capability, which will allow them to analyze our vocal dynamics, pitches, and intonations. They will include all of these factors in their understanding of what we're saying to them. Conversely, to assist us in understanding our VIVOs, researchers have already begun to develop software that will put an animated face, upper body, or full body on each VIVO monitor with its own facial expressions, lip movements, and body language.

Furthermore, we'll develop special abbreviated spoken languages to speed up communication with our talking computers. Just as we created various versions of "shorthand" notation to speed up writing, we'll create spoken "shorttongues." To assist our information searches, non-text visual symbols and oral-aural sound-"icons" will replace written hyperlinks.

My point is that speaking and listening to VIVOs will be both different from and similar to the ways we ordinarily speak and listen in today's text-literate societies. On the one hand, we'll have new 21st Century skills, techniques, and technologies available that will speed up and facilitate spoken communication and information storage-retrieval between people and talking computers. On the other, we'll just think out loud—just converse—with VIVOs as we do now when we talk to other people.

Critique point #3: Much more computer memory is required to store speech than to store text. This will make talking computers too expensive, people won't buy them, and companies and universities won't bother to research and develop them.

Reply to point #3: VIVOs won't be more expensive, and everybody will buy them. The industry is already successfully compressing storage space, making storage of speech more efficient and requiring less memory.

Think, for example, of the way the industry has dealt with the once prohibitively-high cost of storing computer graphics. I'll paraphrase Nicholas Negroponte in his book, *Being Digital*. The more pixels, the more memory you need. A typical screen with

1000 x 1000 pixels in full color needs 24 million bits of memory. In 1961, memory cost $1. per bit. By 1995, 24 million bits of memory cost $60. Speech storage will follow a similar path.

The computer industry is going to continue to research and develop VIVOs and put them on the international market for the same reasons that industries continue to do R and D on any product: the prospect of a huge demand, ready markets, and megaprofits.

VIVOs, being nonliterate-user-friendly, will fit the needs of governments, corporations, businesses, and agencies in countries around the world. The workforces in the great majority of countries—including the electronically-developed countries— are mostly nonliterate or semi-literate. Employers will soon realize that, once they install VIVOs in their facilities, they will be able to open up their information-handler labor pools to nonliterate employees.

Nonliterate individuals will also want VIVOs for their personal use for all the same reasons that literate individuals desire text-driven computers today. And today's literate users will switch to VIVOs tomorrow—as they've already switched to calculators instead of doing arithmetic the old way—because VIVOs will be more efficient, more natural, and less labor-intensive than text-driven computers.

In addition, the computer industry is responding to the fact that literacy rates among young people in the electronically-developed countries remain low. As this customer base of young people settles into the 21st Century, it will seek out, and buy, computers that won't require a familiarity with text.

Finally, echoing a point I made earlier in the book, the computer industry's rush to judgment, as regards its current decision to accelerate research and development of talking computers, is its way of responding—albeit unawares—to the deeper evolutionary pressures mandating that we literates return to our human, biogenetic, oral-aural roots ASAP.

While the above discussion focused on how we'll search for information when we're not sure what's available or exactly what we're looking for, another area of skepticism concerns how we'll use VIVOs to search for information that we've previously accessed and whose aural stream has already passed us by. How will we be able to reaccess information on our VIVOs using only oral-aural means?

How, for instance, will a user indicate to her VIVO computer that she wants to re-hear a ten-second section of voice-out that she heard three minutes ago? The "how" here is connected to the "how" in the question: How will the computer software be set up to measure the flow of its output?

By way of analogy, a book's "output" can be measured in chapters, in numbers of pages, in paragraphs, sentences, and words. If I want to reread a short section that I read three minutes ago, I can usually find the section pretty quickly because, through practice, I've developed some mental correlations between reading time, reading speed, and the location in the book of what I've read. If I know that I've been reading this book at medium (for me) speed with no interruptions for five minutes, then I can take an educated guess regarding how many pages I'll have to flip back to find the section I want to reread.

My mental correlations are based on the technology of bookbinding, which gives me pages to turn, the customs of bookwriting, which give me chapters, and the characteristics of written language, which give me words, sentences, and paragraphs.

But what technology will VIVO computers use in their voice-out operations that will allow me to "paginate" or "chapter" the output? Based on that technology, whatever it will be—plus the natural "word," "sentence," and "paragraph" spacings of *spoken* language—I'll have to develop the necessary mental correlations between the listening time, the speed at which the language is being spoken, and the "location" in the voice-out of the words I want to reaccess.

This will require our developing enhanced time-sound and distance-sound correlation skills—items on our list of VIVOlutionary learning skills.

We're all familiar with one type of indicator for marking time and place on oral outflows. That's the little numerical counter we found on audiocassette players. In the yesteryears of audiocassette players, when we wanted to be able to return to a particular hot moment on our favorite musical group's audio-cassette, we made a mental note of the number that appeared on the counter at that hot moment and, later, rewound the tape until that number reappeared on the counter.

However, our audiocassette player's number counter just won't work as a model for marking our VIVO's oral outflow. We'll need a marker that won't take the form of written numbers or letters.

We can take a clue from the way most of us today search and find particular information on audiotape, and on video-tape and computer screens, too. When we do listen to audiocas-settes, we don't really look at that little number counter anymore. We've learned to correlate the time it takes to rewind a tape with the distance covered on the tape. We use our sense of this correlation to rewind the tape to the approximate location of the hot moment we're seeking. We do the same when we're searching backward and forward through the taped messages on our telephone answering machines.

We have—as anyone who's played tennis, or merely walked across a busy street, knows—an innate ability to correlate amounts of time with distances in space, to function naturally within the four-dimensional space-time continuum. For humans, it's a survival mechanism. Our being able to rewind an audiocassette's tape to an approximate desired location is tied to our biogenetic ability to track down food: we must reach that savanna (or supermarket) and capture food to eat before sundown, or we'll go hungry through the night.

Using VIVOs, we'll rely on our space-time-correlation ability to help us backtrack, relocate, and pounce on spoken information that has already crossed our paths. What technological approaches will we develop to accomplish this? Here are a couple of possibilities, though I'm sure that you, dear reader, can come up with many more.

Regarding time-sound correlations, imagine that my VIVO computer measured voice-out by marking every 250th word with a BEEP (horn), and every 1000th word with a DING (bell). Some of today's text-based software already contain this feature for measuring text flow. Soon I'd become skilled at estimating the number of BEEPS-AGO or DINGS-AGO that I could find a particular section of voice-out. Or perhaps my computer would give a BUZZ every two minutes to help me mark the passage of oral outflow. I'd need to learn to collect and count those BUZZES without breaking my concentration on the voice-out's content.

Regarding distance-sound correlations, think scroll bars. On our wrists, we might wear a watch-sized scroll-bar screen, a visual aid that would contain two parallel scroll bars set to scroll vertically or horizontally, whichever the user preferred. One bar would be voice-activated and, set at a default speed, would measure the user/VIVO-voice flow on a particular project. The other would be a timer, measuring the time flow of a particular project in whatever configuration of units—seconds, minutes, and/or hours—the user preferred.

The wrist scroller, linked to the VIVO by wireless remote, would not just passively measure the voice and time flows of a project, but would allow the user to actively scroll backward and forward through the data, locating yet-to-be-accessed data (YTBAD) and relocating previously-accessed data (PAD). The user would operate each scroll bar by voice commands and/or by touch—moving her fingertip forward and backward along the bar—until she located the desired data.

Of course, the most efficient solution for retrieving spoken information from our VIVO's memory banks would be to take the approach discussed at the beginning of this chapter: to create VIVOs with oral-keyword and TOL capabilities, conversation-friendly computers that would allow me to fall back on the informal techniques for locating information that I use in ordinary spoken conversation.

I might, for example, ask my VIVO, "What was it you said a few minutes ago about Ralph's wanting to find a new apartment?" or "What were you saying a few minutes ago just before you started talking about Ralph's dog?" Assuming my VIVO was still feeling "conversation-friendly," it would tell me.

There's one more critique I'd like to reply to—one that some readers might have already uttered silently to yourselves. If you happened to make this critique using subvocal, subauditory speech, then you've already demonstrated, in practice, one solution to the problem raised by this critique.

The critique: Imagine a roomful of people all chattering away at their VIVOs at the same time—people working in a large office, students studying in a classroom, or a family sharing a home space. What a sonic clash! How will we ever get anything done surrounded by that incessant din?

Relax. Instead of people shouting at their VIVOs, visualize roomfuls of people silently compspeaking.

According to a NASA Ames Research Center report (March 17, 2004) on the work of ARC scientists Dr. Chuck Jorgensen and colleagues: "NASA scientists found that small button-sized sensors stuck under the chin and on either side of the 'Adam's apple,' could gather nerve signals, and send them to a processor and then to a computer program that translates them into words.

"Biological signals arise when reading or speaking to one-self with or without actual lip or facial movement…. A person using the subvocal system thinks of phrases and talks to himself so quietly it cannot be heard, but the tongue and vocal cords do receive speech signals from the brain….

"Eventually, such 'subvocal speech' systems could be used in spacesuits, in noisy places like airport towers, or even in traditional voice-recognition programs…. [P]ersons [with disabilities] could use this system for a lot of things."

Will speaking subvocally, rather than aloud, for much of each day completely satisfy our human, biogenetic need to speak? Will it make us forget how to sound out our languages' words—how to pronounce them aloud and give them proper intonation? Will it be effective in helping to cure our speech-deficiency illness? And will TOS (thinking out subvocally) make TOL obsolete in the VIVO Age, turning conversations with VIVOs into "sounds of silence" and relegating TOL to the museum wall alongside the scythe and the butter churn?

Lots of questions here. We'd better ask our great-great-grandchildren for the answers.

CHAPTER 7

Written Numerals,
Your Number's Up!
And VIVO's Got Your Number!

"Five, seven, eight, clink!, three, zero, nine, (pause), one, six, one, point, two, four, clink!..." My VIVO's throwing more spoken numbers at me than an auctioneer in full flight. Endless strings of numbers—and all I had asked it for was last month's credit card action, including my bank deposits and withdrawals, my house bills, and my purchases.

How in the world will we be able to deal with all these strings of spoken numbers in the years to come? How will we verbally store and retrieve numbers on our VIVOs, when we'll have to deal with strings of numbers as long and complicated as the annual spread sheets of a business, the complex equations of astrophysics, or even our monthly credit card statements?

Yes, it's true that our 21st Century ability for holding strings of spoken numbers, as well as spoken words, in our minds will be much improved over our present, laughable non-ability in this area. After all, practice will make perfect, and our VIVOs will be giving our memories lots of practice.

It's also true that VIVOs will be holding up their end of the bargain by calculating whatever we ask them to calculate—using their internal calculator function—and telling us the results. However, it's clear that we're going to have to take some *extra* steps to help our VIVOs and ourselves deal with storing and receiving spoken numerical information,

In this chapter, I am first going to look at some ways we'll be able to expedite our process of verbally communicating in and about numbers with our VIVOs. Next, I am going to describe some simple *visual* helpmates that will make our life among the spoken numbers a lot easier. I'll end by briefly discussing the sticky question of how people in the 21st Century will do theoretical mathematics in the *absence of* written numerals.

Returning to the question that opened this chapter, does anyone have a clue about how to handle and sort out those long strings of spoken numbers?

Our children, it turns out, are already working on this problem—although mostly unconsciously, and out of a felt need. Though they haven't gotten very far yet, their methods already suggest directions for further exploration.

Many teenagers and younger children do not read the "names" of numbers in the traditional way. If a number like 736,401 pops up on their calculators, and they're asked what number it is, many of them won't say "seven hundred (and) thirty-six thousand, four hundred (and) one." Instead, they'll say "seven, three, six,(pause), four, zero (or 'oh'), one."

What they're really doing—and they've developed this capacity in a mere single generation—is "digitalizing" the reading and writing of all mathematics. Obviously, they've been inspired by their digital watches and all the other digital read-outs in their lives. They've discovered that they only need to know the names of ten numbers (= 0 - 9), or at the very most one hundred-and-one numbers (= 0 - 100), plus "point" for the decimal point and a pause for the comma, to be able to store and retrieve all the mathematical information they feel they'll need in their lives.

Try it yourself. Isn't it much quicker and easier to memorize and say "seven, three, six, (pause), four, oh, one," than "seven hundred (and) thirty-six thousand, four hundred (and) one"? Isn't that why most of us have chosen this same oral-aural format for saying our telephone numbers?

This method also gives us a better chance of clarifying oral-aural ambiguities in spoken numbers, regardless whether it's a person or a VIVO who's speaking the number. If a VIVO said to you, "one hundred seventy thousand one," what number or numbers would you hear?

a. 1 100 70 1000 1
b. 100 70,000 1
c. 170,000 1
d. 170,001

You'd probably ask the VIVO to give you a break, to repeat the number, and to keep it simple. "O.K.," the VIVO would reply: "one, seven, zero, (pause) (= comma), zero, zero, one, clink! (= stop)." Ah, now you'd know that "d" was the answer.

Our children are helping us to see that, in this age of calculators, all of our daily applications of numbers can be—and, in many cases, have already been—reduced to our dealing with strings of "digitalized" numbers. This whole "digitalizing" process created by our children is a transitional procedure, a further step in our evolution from doing math via numeral notational systems, as we've done in the past, to doing math without using any numerals, as we'll do in the future. Once again, wisdom tells us to listen to the children.

Today, our calculators feed us strings of written numerals, calculate what we ask them to calculate, and output their results in the form of more written numerals. However, once we've reconfigured our calculators and other numeral-producing devices to present their information orally instead of as written numerals, we'll be saying "goodbye" to numerals altogether. Written numerals will disappear with the rest of written language in the 21st Century. We'll be left with our VIVOs speaking to us in strings of "digitalized" numbers, complete with pauses, "points," and "clinks!"

There will be those 21st Century occasions, however, when trying to hold long strings of numbers in our minds, even simplified "digitalized" strings, just won't work. We're going to need to add some visual aids to our arsenal. Welcome to the Land of LORNS!

You get on your pushbutton phone, and you make a call to a number that you call frequently. Maybe it's a number that belongs to your best friend, your life partner, a son or daughter, a close co-worker at your workplace. You know the call I mean—the one where you don't have to think about or consciously remember the phone number before you push the buttons, the one where your fingers seem to "do the walking" on their own.

How is this possible? You've memorized a pattern of button-pushing operations that stays with you in your mind, in your vision, and in your muscles, and you're able to use this pattern even when you're not actually thinking about the phone number itself. By now, you might have even forgotten what the phone number was—but you sure can dial it quickly without a second thought. In some cases, if I asked you what that number was, you might first have to watch your fingers walk through their pattern, noticing which buttons they pushed, before you could tell me the number.

If you're someone whose fingers sometimes seem to switch to automatic pilot in the way I just described, then congratulations! You're starting to become an expert at manipulating the world of the 21st Century—at least that part that deals with numbers. For the button pattern you've memorized already qualifies you as a LORNS semi-pro.

For most of our daily 21st Century work-a-day routine, whenever we'll need visual-display back-up for spoken numbers, we'll turn to LORNS. LORNS are location relative numeral substitutes (a term coined by the author), simplified visual signs or symbols that do the jobs that written numerals do for us today, but more quickly and efficiently, requiring less concentration and work. Let's look at how LORNS work.

Every evening you call your best friend Kaneesha to chat. Usually when you punch in her number, 402-371-5869, you do it so quickly that you're almost always unaware of doing it. But this time, when you select Kaneesha's number, make yourself

[1]

[2]

aware of the pattern your hand follows. We'll start with a representation of the standard pushbutton phone numeral grid design (Figure 1), and add lines indicating the pattern your hand follows to dial Kaneesha's number (Figure 2).

We've broken the phone number and overall hand pattern into four distinct hand operations: 402, 371, 58, and 69. These four operations are represented in Figure 2 by lines connecting the numbers. The first number, or starting point, of each operation is indicated by the little dot at the tip of each line. The length of the "dashes" making up the lines indicates the order of the four operations. We read the lines made up by the shortest "dashes" first, then those with the next longest "dashes," and so on, in sequence, until we reach the lines with the longest "dashes."

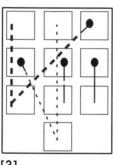

[3]

To create a true LORNS from Figure 2, we need to drop the numerals and letters entirely out of the picture. We'll retain the phone's pushbutton grid and base our recognition of this LORNS on the location of the lines relative to the grid. The result is Figure 3. Figure 3 is what your button-pushing hand seems to know how to do on its own when you call Kaneesha.

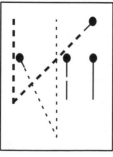

[4]

Lastly, by dropping out the representations of the pushbuttons, and just keeping the grid's frame, we get Figure 4. By the time we get to Figure 4, we've eliminated written numerals, and we've proven we don't need written numerals to store and retrieve phone numbers.

Figure 4 is really a hieroglyph of Kaneesha's phone number. If I asked you to write down her number for me so that I could call her later, you could just sketch this hieroglyph and hand it to me. All LORNS are numerical hieroglyphs.

If you've stayed with the discussion to this point, you're probably muttering to yourself that it's a heck of a lot easier to just write and read 402-371-5869 than to write and read that damn LORNS. True, it may be easier for us, with our vast experience manipulating written numerals, but it won't be easier for our great-great-grandchildren, who will not have experienced that experience. Let's see, however, if we can create a simpler, more intuitive LORNS system here.

We can create a LORNS that represents Kaneesha's phone number by substituting dots for the numerals. We'll again use the pushbutton phone grid as our launching pad. We'll locate the dots in their squares relative to their locations in the phone grid as shown in Figure 5.

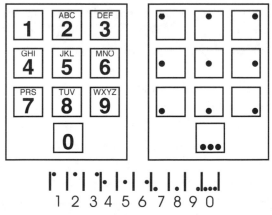

[5]

Now if we start with a horizontal matrix pre-divided into equal, adjoining squares, we can write Kaneesha's phone number like this: ⊦ ⌐⌐⏌˙⏌ ˙⏌. ⌐ ⏌˙⏌.⏌ ⊣ ⌐.

We can also use this LORNS system to write her birthdate: ⌐⌐⌐.⏌ ˙⌐⌐⊦ ⏌. ⏌ , her Social Security number: ⏌ ⌐.⏌. ⊦-⏌ ⊣˙⏌-⊦⏌ ˙⏌˙⌐ ⏌, the time of day: ⌐ ⏌˙⏌˙⏌ ⌐ , and any other series of numbers we have to write.

Once we learn to read and write this LORNS system, it's definitely easier and quicker than reading and writing numerals. In fact, almost anything is easier than reading and writing numerals. All those curves, lines, loops, and squiggles to attend to! Reading and writing numerals requires significantly more visual effort, mental concentration, muscular coordination (if handwriting them), time, and patience than reading and writing the dots in this second LORNS system.

Crossman's Law says: if it's cheaper and more profitable to produce, and quicker and easier for consumers to use, it'll probably happen. Because of Crossman's Law, technology developers in the first quarter of the 21st Century will begin to replace numerals with LORNS—either the LORNS system I've just described or some other LORNS system that's even more cost- and use-efficient. Look for calculators with LORNS read-outs in the sale bins of your local Wal-Mart by Year 2015.

What makes both systems of LORNS depicted above understandable to us is that they're based on the familiar pushbutton phone grid. A unique phenomenon of all LORNS systems is that, after a generation or two, people using a particular LORNS system will no longer be aware of that *original* grid, function, and operations of the system they're using.

A child in Year 2020, using a voice-driven calculator with the second LORNS system above, probably won't realize that the positions of its dots correspond to the locations of the numbered buttons on a pushbutton phone grid. Chances are they will have never used, or even seen, a device that is merely a telephone. Telephony will be integrated into their VIVOs, without a numeral—or pushbutton—in sight.

The phrase "to *punch in* a phone number" will have as little meaning to a child in 2020 as the phrase "to *dial* a phone number" has to a child today. In fact, since voice "dialing" is already being offered by the phone companies, push button phones are already antiques!

Is it important that children of the future be aware of the origins of their VIVO's LORNS system(s) in order to use it effectively? Not at all.

Nowadays, we use LORNS all the time without thinking about their original (but now absent) numeral displays and grid frames. The fuel gauges in our cars are LORNS.

Most of us probably don't know the capacity of our car's fuel tank in numbers of gallons or liters. Unless we're figuring the exact amount of money we're spending on fuel, or planning a trip where there are few gas stations, we don't need to know what number of gallons the "F" or the lines on the gauge represent.

We don't need numerals across the gauge that tell us we have ten gallons of fuel left. That's been calibrated and configured for us by automotive engineers. It's enough that we know the *relative* amount of fuel we have in our tank.

As LORNS lose their original operational meanings—their references and links to numerals—they'll become more and more self-referential entities. One more example: the more

that I and other people in the future store, retrieve, and communicate our Personal Identity LORNS, the less I and the rest of the world will remember that these LORNS used to represent numerals: specifically, the numerals of what we used to call our "Social Security Number." Like my voiceprint, my fingerprint, my eye's iris-print, and my DNA map, my Personal Identity LORNS will just be another symbol or picture that represents *me*.

Our great-great-grandchildren might very well live their whole lives without ever reading, writing, learning, or even seeing written numerals. Whenever they'll need visual representations of the numbers they're storing and retrieving, they'll turn to LORNS for assistance. As they move closer toward an oral culture, they'll do more and more of their applied math orally-aurally and rely less and less on visual aids like LORNS. They'll just think their math questions and problems out loud (TOL) to their VIVOs, and their VIVOs will TOL the answers back to them.

Historically, before we wrote today's numerals, we represented numbers using other numeral systems, such as these cuneiform characters for the numbers 1 through 10:

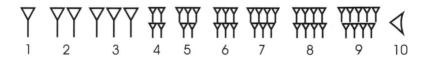

Eventually, we replaced those hieroglyphs with the Arabic numeral system that we use today. In the 21st Century, we'll reverse this process by replacing Arabic numerals with a new family of hieroglyphs: LORNS.

In short, we'll be deconstructing our numeral system in stages that reflect its original construction, but in reverse order. Another technology-sponsored, forward-to-the-past phenomenon.

Graphs can easily replace numerals in all digital displays. Bar charts, pie charts, and ogives (cumulative line graphs) become LORNS once we remove all their numerals and define their parameters and an operation for them to perform.

The numerals on graphs indicate absolute amounts or percentages; numeral-less graphs indicate relative amounts or percentages. We already know how to make this absolute-to-relative shift mentally; we do it whenever we look at our cars' fuel gauges. But in the VIVO Age, we're really going to have to develop this shifting skill.

A LORNS of today that I find particularly interesting is the watchface with hands but no numerals. It works for us because we're still aware of the positions where numerals are usually located on standard watchface grids. And we use the winder knob's placement alongside the watchface to tell us where the "12" and "6" should be.

Numeral-less bar graph

[7]

Now that numerals are disappearing from watches with faces, how long will it be before numerals also start disappearing from *digital* watches?

Digital watches have become the watch of choice for today's younger generation. But why has it taken so long for digital watches and clocks to become commonplace in our society? Why has the watchface with hands pointing to numerals around the face's circumference ruled us for so long?

It's not because we had to wait for the era of electronics. When I was a child, I had a mechanical wind-up clock that displayed time in digits, the way digital watches do today. My guess at an answer: the face and hands of watches represent our timekeeping heritage. They echo and maintain for us our ancient connection with the sundial, and it has been difficult for us to say "goodbye" to this icon of our past.

Our move to digital watches and clocks has signified a radical philosophical break in the way we literally *look* at time. (Why do you think it's called a "watch"?) On the traditional watchface, we can simultaneously see all the hours represented by numerals. We can see the past, where the hands have already pointed, and the future, where the hands will point, as well as the present, where they are pointing now. Watchfaces depict time as a river flowing in a smooth, unbroken course from past to present to future.

Digital watch displays, however, show us only one set of four numerals peeping through fixed windows. They're capable of representing only one frozen moment at a time. Unlike watchfaces, they don't let us view the past-present-future sweep of time. Consequently, digital watches are compelled to depict time as merely a succession of *present moments*, as having no past and no future. The message of this digital medium is that there's no history—nothing worth remembering—and nothing to plan for.

To the extent that technology, in this case the technology we use to keep time, both reflects and shapes the ways we think and act, we're quickly becoming a society that lives in the *digital now*—in the present, for the present. The political, ethical, and psychological implications of this are worth a ponder or two.

I want to end this chapter by briefly addressing the question that inevitably gets asked wherever I speak about our transition to an oral culture. How will mathematicians, physicists, and the like perform the tasks of theoretical mathematics without using written numerals? Won't they continue to require written numerals to do their complex, complicated work?

To be honest, I don't know the answer to this question. I'm not an expert in theoretical mathematics, and even if I were, I think it would be difficult to predict which formats future mathematicians et al will actually use to carry on mathematical inquiry, construct proofs, and solve problems.

In the 1997 film *Good Will Hunting*, audiences full of non-mathematicians like myself watched as a young, self-taught math prodigy solved a difficult chalkboard problem in a specialty area of geometry known as combinatorics. The problem appeared on the board in the form of a spider-like diagram containing no numerals. In solving the problem, the young man extended the diagram in certain ways, but added no numerals.

We, the audience, were catching a brief glimpse of a type of theoretical mathematics that seems to have eliminated written numerals entirely. If it is possible in this one area of mathematics, isn't it possible in others? Surely the field of theoretical mathematics will be entering new universes of language systems, both visual and oral, in the 21st Century that today's mathematicians themselves can only barely glimpse—or not glimpse at all.

One thing I am sure about is that theoretical mathematicians in the VIVO Age won't utilize today's written numerals as visual representations of numbers. Numerals, as I've said, are just too slow and inefficient a way to store and retrieve mathematical information. Those working in higher mathematics will create their own LORNS systems—systems that probably will *not* have sprung from pushbutton phone grids.

CHAPTER 8

How I Un(w)rote the Notes: Retooling the Arts to Fit an Oral Culture

When I was eight, I started piano lessons with Miss Charlotte. What happened at my first lesson? Miss Charlotte opened my *Diller-Quaile 1st Solo Book for Piano* to page one. First, she taught me to recognize the treble and bass clefs as they appeared on the page. Then, she taught me to read the "middle C" note just below the treble clef. Finally, she taught me to locate the "middle C" note on the piano keyboard.

In the following weeks and months, Miss Charlotte taught me many more notes by first teaching me their written location on the staffs/staves and then teaching me their actual location on the keyboard. With each new note that I learned, I would also learn to read and play a new little song that incorporated that new note in its melody. This is pretty typical of the way most children are taught to play piano and other instruments in the print-literate countries. They learn to read the notes, and then they learn to apply what they've read to their instruments.

But what is really going on inside this activity we call "music lessons"? What was really being communicated when Miss Charlotte, each Tuesday from 5:00 till 5:30 p.m., earnestly tried to teach me to play the piano?

Miss Charlotte, it turns out, was teaching me a new language called "music." It's actually three different languages: an oral-aural language of sounds—the actual music; a written language of symbols that represents the sounds—the written score; and a spoken language of words that is used to describe aloud the heard sounds and to read aloud the written score (if there is a written score).

Each of these three languages called "music" has its own vocabulary. Each portrays rhythm, harmony, melody, and dynamics in its own way. In learning the first language of music, I was learning to hear and recognize the sounds made by an instrument when it played or by a voice when it sang. What fun I had singing tunes that I had learned or just heard, picking out the tunes on the piano "by ear," and tapping my feet to the rhythms!

In learning music's second language, I was learning to read and write notes, time signatures, chord signatures, key signatures, pitch notations, velocity and dynamics notations—all the signatures and notations in which the musical sounds were stored.

Thirdly, I was learning to be able to say what sounds I was hearing and/or what written notations and signatures I was reading and writing.

In addition to learning these three new music languages, I was also learning how to bundle them together and apply them by learning to play actual tunes on the piano. This required my developing other special skills, like being able to perceive, by eye and by hand, the arrangement of notes on the sheet music and keys on the keyboard, and being able to push down the keys strongly or lightly on command.

I've already gotten more technical here than I'd intended. The point I want to draw from recounting my first piano lesson is that, at age eight, I was being taught three new music-related languages and how to apply them. That's quite a load for anyone of any age to learn. It required reading, writing, listening, speaking, and playing in what were actually three new "foreign" languages. It required constant, instantaneous translation from one of these languages into one or both of the others. It even required new applications of math to interpret the time signatures, count the beats per measure, and add up the time values of the notes.

No wonder some piano teachers I've talked with recommend waiting until a child is eight-years-old to begin lessons. As one piano teacher said to me recently, a child's successful entrance into the world of piano lessons requires their having already reached a certain level of "maturity"—that is, a degree of experience and development in language and math, in reading, writing, and speaking.

Interestingly, according to this piano teacher, it's not the physical manipulation of the piano keys that requires this "maturity." The tiny hands of a four-year-old child can accomplish a surprising array of piano-playing techniques. Hand size can adapt to technique, and technique can adapt to hand size. Miss Charlotte herself, a family friend, recommended that I waited until I was eight to begin my piano lessons. Now I realize why: because in the tradition of most music instruction in Western countries, she wanted me to be able to *read and write* the music I'd be playing.

But if a child can start learning to read and write in their native language at age five or six, why wait until age eight to begin music lessons? Why not start teaching them music at five or six also?

I'll paraphrase another music teacher's answer: it's not good to try to teach a child to play an instrument at the same time that the child is starting to learn to read and write in school. There are just too many different kinds of reading and writing going on—too many written languages being learned simultaneously. The child might hit "overload" and get unnecessarily discouraged and depressed about playing their instrument. That teacher's advice: wait till the child is "over the first hump" of learning to read and write their native language; then, get her started playing music.

Still another music teacher friend also agrees that starting to teach a child of five or six to play an instrument is a mistake for the reason just mentioned. However, this teacher recommends teaching a child the languages of music at ages three or four, *before* she learns to read and write in school—*before* "the hump."

Let's tie all this into our own journey toward an oral culture. Written language, using an alphabet or other forms, is just one of our many written information storage and retrieval systems. Music notation, using staffs/staves and notes, is another. The composer/arranger freezes musical information onto the page using notes, and the musician thaws it out by reading and playing it. Dance movement notational systems such as Labanotation store the choreographer's dance sequences on the page for the dancer to retrieve and follow.

I'm not sure about the future of Labanotation, but I am sure that our traditional notes-on-staff music notation is headed for extinction as VIVO technology reshapes human society in the 21st Century.

How many people in countries that rely strongly upon music notation *haven't* studied, played, or composed music because they were deterred by having to learn and master *reading* music? Or, how many people, discouraged, quit after several months of music lessons? Most young people, already turned off by trying to learn to read and write in school, have not been enthusiastic about the prospect of trying to learn yet another notational system.

As with all notational systems, including text/written language, music notation serves to divide community: those who can write and read it from those who can't. Those who can write and read music notation—the composers, the arrangers, the performers—receive the accolades and the "perks." Those who lack the notation skills comprise their audience.

And as with written language, some people promote and profit from the division between the musically literate and the musically nonliterate, between the musical "cans" and the musical "can'ts." If everyone could engage in that activity we call "playing music," then the "star" system that supports CD, concert, video, Internet, and sheet music sales would disappear. It would be replaced by millions of composers, bands, and individuals making music.

Some of these millions of music-makers would be making wonderful music, and some not. Some would be experts by today's commercial standards, and some not. But all of them would be *creating*—actively, not passively, participating in a worldwide wave of music-making. Each person would have the option to create music, or listen to others create it, or both.

Music would become a two-way interface involving all members of a community, not just one-way from the "stars" to the rest of us. In this way, music, like our spoken language, would deepen its original role as part of the glue holding a community together.

Note reading is rote reading. Learning to read musical notes doesn't teach the internal "grammar" or deep structure of music any more than learning to read individual words teaches the deep structure of language.

From knowing how to pronounce the sounds of the written ancient Greek and Hebrew alphabets, I can read and pronounce individual ancient Greek and Hebrew words. But I don't know what most of those words mean, and I can't generate a new sentence of my own in those languages. A classical pianist can sight-read a written transcription of a blues pianist's solo yet still have no idea of the deep structure of the blues or how to generate a blues solo of their own.

Traditional note/staff music notation is starting to disappear as our culture's *essential* method of storing and retrieving musical information. Many composers around the world composing in the Western classical tradition have already been experimenting with new notational language systems to better depict their compositions. As is true with mathematics, newly-created musical wines are requiring newly-designed bottles.

But I see these new music-notational languages as a next-to-last step in a journey to yet a further and final destination: a total oral-aural approach to composing, arranging, and playing music.

In oral cultures, music, like language, was/is passed on from person to person through the memory method of storage and retrieval. One person plays or sings the music for others until the latter remember how to play or sing it; then, the latter play or sing it for others who learn it by listening and watching, and so on.

It's the apprenticeship method of learning an art or a craft. People learn music by listening, watching, and playing or singing, not by reading. Imagine taking this person-to-person method and implementing it using VIVO computers together with videos, holograms, CD-ROMs, etc., and we get a sense of how, in our soon-to-be oral culture, the old will become new again.

Imagine if Miss Charlotte had gone about teaching me to play piano in an entirely different way. Imagine that, instead of first opening the *Diller-Quaile* book and pointing out the "middle C" note written on page one, she had told me to sit beside her at the keyboard, watch her hands, and listen as she played a song over several times. Imagine that, after playing the song, she had asked me to play the same song, either by myself or together with her. This would be teaching by showing and involving the student; it would be learning by listening, watching, and copying the teacher.

It would be the same method used to teach and learn music, and almost everything else, in most nonliterate societies. Two of the languages of music would be operative here: the piano's sounds, and our spoken descriptions of the piano's sounds. The third language, the written representation of the piano's sounds, would have no place in this scenario.

This is what I imagine piano lessons of the future will be like—because this is what I imagine *music-making* of the future will be like: no reading, no writing, just the sounds of people playing instruments and voices singing and talking.

It could be that the Miss Charlottes of the 21st Century won't even be sitting there on the piano benches next to their students. We already have piano teachers instructing students via video and the Internet, but we can certainly construct more imaginative scenarios of things to come.

Maybe the piano student will just slip on a pair of electronically-controlled robotic gloves that will guide their hands through the playing of the tune—until they're able to play it without the gloves. Or maybe the student will match their own hand movements to the movements of a pair of holographic "hands," whose images will be superimposed over their hands on the keyboard.

In any case, the child of the future who wants to play music won't have to face the daunting prospect of learning to read and write music in order to play it. Without the constraints of reading and writing music, and with the essence of their music-making once again located in their production of musical sounds, the child will, I believe, experience a level of joy in their piano lessons that I found missing in mine.

This production-of-musical-sounds approach will also predispose the child toward musical *improvisation*. For the first time since music notation demolished it in the musically "literate" countries of the West, improvised music, I believe, will once again become universally embraced as a legitimate form of music-making.

Bach, Mozart, Beethoven—all were great improvisers in the European classical tradition and included improvised passages in their compositions. But the Western classical musical establishment soon wrung improvisation out of its repertoire and scorned other world musics that were based on improvisation. In the 21st Century, musical traditions of improvised music— jazz and the blues are two examples—will finally gain the respect they deserve.

As in the past, music will be of, by, and for the people—each society a musical democracy (unlike the musical autocracy the West has become). The concept of music as "art," practiced only by those literate in music notation, will give way to music as a necessarily participatory activity involving all members of society.

The Internet has already begun to blur the division between professional, upper-case "C" Composers and the lower-case "c" folks who want to create their own music and disseminate it to their friends and/or to the world. Today, anyone, including people who can't read a note of music, can create music by singing or playing an instrument, digitizing the sound, uploading it to an Internet site, and zooming it to (potentially) billions of ears.

What would our great-great-grandchild's first piano teacher, a VIVO-Age Miss Charlotte, think about all this? She'd probably heave a huge sigh of relief and say, "That poor, poor 20th Century Charlotte, having to teach all that note reading." And she'd add, "What fun I have teaching kids to create and sing tunes, pick them out "by ear" on their electronic keyboards, and tap their feet to the rhythms!"

Extend this 21st Century musical model to other arts that currently rely on writing and reading: novels, poetry, short stories, plays, and screenplays. Before written language, the ancestral forms of novels, poetry, and the rest were oral-aural in nature and utilized the memory method of storing and retrieving their information. Those people who knew and gave voice to a society's accumulated wisdom became its griots, storytellers, shamans, poets, troubadours, blues singers, and rappers.

Anyone who could speak—that is, almost everyone—might become a griot in their own community or family. This wasn't some narrow category of "art-speak"; this was "survival-speak," "history-speak," "feelings-speak," "spirits-speak," "life-speak." How this has changed as we have evolved into a print-literate society where only the highly literate are allowed to tell their stories—to disseminate their "art"—to the community through their novels, short stories, essays, plays, and poetry!

Imagine only *listening* to "novels," poems, stories, and play "scripts" instead of reading them. Imagine all of us "life-speaking" them ourselves: repeating those of others and/or creating our own with the help of our talking computers.

What has been happening to poetry in many print-literate countries in the last decade gives us clues to the new direction. We've seen the explosive proliferation of public poetry readings, where poetry is *recited*, and the equally explosive emergence of "performance" poetry, which presents poetry combined with theater, music, and/or dance in public performance.

In poetry "circuses" and "slams," poets compete by reciting their poems, often improvising new poems on the spot, in front of boisterous audiences. Rap—the "performance" poetry of Black communities—is influencing cultures worldwide. Spoken-word concerts abound. Monologuists are finding receptive audiences. "Open mike" nights at neighborhood clubs allow everyone the chance to become apprentice-griots.

Taken together, these happenings define a trend: the oralizing-auralizing and democratizing of literature, leading to a *world* of poets and storytellers.

Regarding the visual arts, today's artists, from painters and printmakers to digital artists and holographers, have a VIVO-inspired 21st Century surprise waiting for them. Increasingly, they've been incorporating text/written words into the visual designs of their works. The result is that these words introduce some level of *semantic meaning* into the overall visual designs— which, in most cases, is what the artists intended.

The surprise is that, as we move toward an oral culture, these incorporated textual elements will lose their semantic relevance entirely and become solely graphic-design elements of the artworks. Why? Because by 2050, almost no one looking at an artwork containing text will be able to read the text or understand what it means or says.

Surely some mid-21st Century artists will continue the trend, popular with past and present artists, of borrowing ancient or contemporary visual symbols and integrating them into their artworks. These artists might even choose "old" alphabetic letters (a, b, c), written numbers (1, 2, 3), or pictographs-hieroglyphs as their symbols. However, if they do, most of the VIVO-Age viewers of their works—and perhaps some of the artists themselves—won't have a clue as to the meanings of those symbols. This is not a surprise.

Do most of today's viewers recognize antiquated symbols embedded in artworks for what they are and understand their meanings? If the ancient cuneiform numeral for "4," depicted in Chapter 7, were dropped into an artwork today, we'd probably mistake it for a group of mushrooms.

Since we wouldn't recognize it as a numeral representing "4," we'd certainly miss any inherent semantic meaning which this numeral "4" carried and introduced into this artwork. Many ancient societies venerated "4" as an expression of the four directions and, therefore, of the totality of all that exists—including all of what we today might call both the physical and spiritual realms. Ooops, and we thought it was just a bunch of mushrooms!

CHAPTER 9

Rereading that Middle Passage: Saying Goodbye to "Standard" Written Languages as Tools of Cultural Domination

O ne of the results of the electronically-developed countries' becoming oral cultures is that they will no longer be able to use their "standard" written languages to culturally dominate other nations and communities. This might sound like small potatoes, but it's actually big potatoes—and hot potatoes.

To illustrate this point, I'll discuss the African-European politico-linguistic dynamic in the United States from the slavery period until the present. I've chosen this example because it allows me to focus on the language(s) and the country I know best—English(es) and the United States. However, what I'll be saying about this example is, in many ways, *applicable worldwide, wherever there are oppressor and oppressed nations and communities*—which is almost everywhere.

During the period of slavery in the U.S., the white

slaveholder encouraged or required the African people he held in bondage to speak his language (English, German, French, Spanish, Dutch, Portuguese, et al) but discouraged or forbade them from learning to read and write it. Why?

This may be the most important question in the world regarding how racism, dominance, language, and technology intersect or, stated more specifically, how literacy intersects the relationship between the oppressor and the oppressed. If we can, in this one brief chapter, begin to sketch an answer to this question, we'll begin to understand *what else* the dominant, electronically-developed nations of the world will be losing when they lose written language in the 21st Century.

To simplify things, let's divide this "Why?" question into two. First, why were captive Africans forced to learn the *spoken* language of the white slaveholder, and what happened when they did? And, second, why weren't captive Africans allowed to learn the *written* language of the white slaveholder, and what happened when some individual Africans finally did?

The Spoken-Language Question

It's not news that many oppressed linguistic communities around the world have been forcibly deprived of their languages by their oppressors. In some cases, it has been their spoken languages only, because they had no written languages. In other cases, where they had both spoken and written languages, they've been deprived of both. Why?

Depriving a linguistic community of its language deprives it of its history, its culture, its ability to build and maintain community. Communication—with its attendant methods of storing and retrieving information—is a necessary condition of human community and culture. When people can communicate, store, retrieve, and share information, the possibility arises for them to link their lives together into a self-determining entity, a community or nation, that can develop and transmit culture in order to survive and thrive. The ability to communicate empowers people and unites their community.

That's why those in power have historically tried to limit communication among the powerless to only those matters that fed the interests of the powerful. On the slave ships, European and U.S. slavetraders took pains to chain an African from one language group to an African from a different language group, so that they would be less able to conspire together.

Once in the "New World," the Africans were forbidden to play the drum, for the drum was integral to communication in many Black African cultures. They were also commonly forbidden to dance their native dances, worship in their native religions, and converse in their native languages. And they were forbidden to learn to read and write. If Africans were caught trying to become literate, they faced death. White people who attempted to teach Africans to read and write might have faced jail for their "crime."

Language is a vehicle for transmitting values. For oppressed communities, language can transmit either the values of empowerment, unity, self-determination, and independence, or else the values of capitulation and acquiescence to the status quo. It's a "power thing."

When one linguistic community goes to school and is taught its lessons in another linguistic community's "standard" spoken and written languages, that reflects which community has the power. That's why, before South Africa's independence, the white apartheid government required Black children to use the "standard" White Afrikaans language in school. It's also why Blacks,

Latinos, Indigenous Peoples, Asians, and other People of Color in the U.S. are required to learn only "standard" White English in school.

Why, then, did the white slaveholders force all captive Africans to learn to speak English (or other European languages)? True, the slaveholders needed to communicate their work orders to the Africans, but that doesn't really answer the question. A slaveholder (or overseer or foreman on larger plantations) could have simply taught a bit of English to just one trusted African under his control, had that African pass on the daily orders to the others by way of African languages and/or gestures, and left it at that. If the slaveholder had left it at that, his life—in the short run—would have been easier. He wouldn't have had to teach all of the other Africans English or police the ban against their using their native African languages.

The slaveholder, however, couldn't and didn't leave it at that. All of the Africans had to learn to speak English so that they—and their children and grandchildren—*wouldn't* speak their *native* languages. Without their native languages, the slaveholder hoped, the Africans would be deprived of their roots, their culture, their very identities.

In place of these, they'd be inoculated with the values of Europe and Christianity that are carried within the English language itself. They'd understand the European rationale for their (the Africans') low station in the "hierarchy of Being" in the "New World," and *they'd come to accept it.*

Ossie Davis, distinguished actor and playwright, eloquently elaborates this point in his essay, "The English Language is My Enemy"—(from *Revelations: An Anthology of Expository Essays By and About Blacks*). "A superficial examination of Roget's *Thesaurus of the English Language* reveals the following facts: the word WHITENESS has 134 synonyms, 44 of which are favorable and pleasing to contemplate, i.e., purity, cleanness, honorable, upright, just, straightforward, fair, genuine, trustworthy.... The word BLACKNESS has 120 synonyms, 60 of which are distinctly unfavorable, and none of them even mildly positive....evil, wicked, malignant, deadly, unclean, dirty, unwashed, foul, and so forth...any teacher good or bad, white or black, Jew or Gentile, who uses the English Language as a medium of communication is forced, willy-nilly, to teach the Negro child 60 ways to despise himself, and the white child 60 ways to aid and abet him in the crime.

"Who speaks to me in my Mother Tongue damns me indeed! ...the English Language—in which I cannot conceive my self as a black man without, at the same time, debasing myself...my enemy, with which to survive at all I must continually be at war."

Furthermore, and equally important, the slaveholder had to force the kidnapped Africans to speak the slaveholder's language so that the Africans' opportunities for *secrecy* would be reduced. Noted author James Baldwin speaks to this in his essay, "If Black English Isn't a Language, Then Tell Me, What Is?"—(from *Revelations: An Anthology of Expository Essays By and About Blacks*).

Arguing that Black English, or Ebonics, is a genuine, authentic language, on a par with "standard" or White English, Baldwin writes, *"A language comes into existence by means of brutal necessity, and the rules of the language are dictated by what the language must convey."*

"There was a moment, in time, and in this place, when my brother, or my mother, or my father, or my sister, had to convey to me, for example, the danger in which I was standing from the white man standing just behind me, and to convey this with a speed, and in a language, that the white man could not possibly understand, and that, indeed, he cannot understand, until today."

The slaveholders had identified and understood a historically key social function of spoken languages. *Spoken languages unite us, bring us together.* Having our own spoken language is a major ingredient in the glue that binds us into a cultural community.

Slaveholders thrust spoken English into captive Africans' minds the way a chemist thrusts a pipette into fluids in a chemistry lab: to draw the Africans' minds away from their original cultural communities and relocate them into new cultural communities of slavery. Slave ships, guns, and whips alone could not have accomplished this task. The English language's role in this forced acculturation process shouldn't be underestimated.

Members of oppressed communities may refuse at first to learn the spoken language of their oppressors, but often, as time goes on and generations pass, they eventually adapt to the oppressive reality of their situation by merging aspects of the oppressors' spoken languages with their own spoken languages, creating totally new, discrete languages. Originally "hybrids," these newly created languages—which (sometimes disparagingly) have been called "Pidgin," "Creole," or "Patois"—often superseded and even replaced completely the oppressed communities' original native languages.

This hybridization, this merging process, is analogous to the way enslaved African communities throughout the Western Hemisphere maintained their native spiritual beliefs in the face of slaveholder prohibitions. By merging certain external elements of the slaveholders' Christian religions with their own African spiritual beliefs, the Africans developed such hybrid religions as

Santeria, Vodou, Condombole, and Kumina.

Varieties of Pidgin arose along the West African coasts and rivers as Europeans needed a way to verbally control, manipulate, and do business with Africans in the context of the slave trade. Pidgin, which is still spoken in some coastal areas of West Africa, is a hybrid of spoken English(es), the languages of coastal West Africa, and other European languages.

The hybrid Gullah language of the Georgia, Florida, and Carolina Sea Islands derives from Pidgin. Africans who remained on, or escaped to, the Sea Islands continued to blend elements of English(es) and other European languages and Pidgin(s) with their native African languages to create Gullah. Then, as U.S. whites purchased Africans as slaves and relocated them throughout the South, North, and Midwest, Pidgin and Gullah accumulated more English and other European linguistic elements and evolved into varieties of Plantation Creole. Today's varieties of spoken Black English are descended from this African-Pidgin-Gullah-Plantation Creole line.

This creating of hybrid languages has been central to U.S. linguistic history, reflecting this country's legacy of slavery, conquest, genocide, domestic colonialism, war, forced land annexation, and segregation, as well as its voluntary immigration patterns. As a result, these hybrid languages house a volatile contradiction within them. For an oppressed community that speaks such a language, the act of speaking it is a badge of both shame and pride.

On the one hand, it is a daily reminder to the oppressed community of its subjugation and the loss of its own native language(s) and culture(s). On the other hand, it is a symbol of the community's resistance against the oppressor, of its commitment to survive by maintaining elements of its own culture(s) and language(s) in spite of the environment of oppression. Whether it's the Gullah language of the Sea Islands, the Black Englishes of Atlanta and Oakland, or the "Spanglishes" of East Los Angeles and Spanish Harlem, the insistent use of such a hybrid language by an oppressed community is a daily expression of its desire for self-determination.

The Written-Language Question

Why weren't enslaved Africans allowed to learn the written language(s) of the white slaveholders, and what happened when some individual Africans finally did?

Spoken English and written English have walked different paths through U.S. history. This country is a polyglot, containing hundreds, maybe thousands, of different community-based spoken Englishes or English-based languages, plus hundreds, maybe thousands, of community-based non-English spoken languages. Yet—no surprise—there is *only one "standard" written* English available to, and imposed upon, all: the written English we all learn in school.

Listen to the many languages we speak: Indigenous/Native Nations' languages, the many native languages of non-English-speaking communities (Spanish, Cantonese, Mandarin, et al), White Englishes, Black Englishes, "Spanglishes," "Frenglishes," (every immigrant community has its own "glishes"), various Patois, Pidgin, and Creole languages. In addition, there are the regional variations of these, the dialects, the street "slangs," and so on. Then look at the way we're taught to write: the "correct" way, the dictionary way, the grammar book way.

Here's an experiment for students to try in school. Write your next essay in a Black English or a "Spanglish," and see what happens! Only "standard" White written English can provide the magic words for information storage and retrieval in U.S. schools, businesses, the media, government institutions, and the professions. Any linguistic community in the U.S. that wants to access stored information must first learn to write "abracadabra" in "standard" English.

Why is this so? Why is there only one "correct" way to write English? Why do our schools and other institutions work so hard to preserve the purity of this written "standard"? Only if "standard" written English remains pure in form can it completely and correctly convey the content that the dominant European-American community intends to convey to all, but especially to the oppressed Communities of Color in the U.S.

What is that content? It's that there is one, and only one, dominant cultural community—the European-Americans'. Whenever an oppressed community is forced to write in the European-Americans' "standard" written language, it's a confirmation, a substantiation, of that content. It's the living proof that European-Americans remain dominant.

The form and content of a language can be separated in abstraction, but not in reality. Mess with the medium (the form), and you mess with the message (the content) itself. If an oppressed community in the U.S. were to succeed in hybridizing "standard" written English, it would effectively belie that written language's content; it would undercut the oppressor's claim to dominance.

The dominant white community in the U.S. isn't pleased that oppressed communities in the U.S. have been able to take "standard" White *spoken* English, blend it with their native languages, and create hybrid spoken languages. But it's too late; there's really nothing that the dominant community can do anymore to prevent that. The dominant community does believe, however, that it still has time to save its "standard" *written* language from hybridization. It has drawn a line in the sand and is saying, "Don't cross!"

Here's a worthy example. Robert L. Steinback, columnist for the *Miami Herald*, wrote an Op-Ed piece, which appeared in the *Atlanta Constitution*, Oct. 5, 1993, criticizing a new book which had translated the first five books of the *Old Testament* of the *Bible* into a particular variety of Black English. The book, by P. K. McCary, is titled *Black Bible Chronicles: From Genesis To The Promised Land/Book One.*

McCary rewrites the first verses of the "Book of Genesis" as follows: "Now when the Almighty was first down with His program, He made the heavens and the earth. The earth was a fashion misfit, being so uncool and dark, but the Spirit of the Almighty came down real tough...."

Steinback comments, "At best, this book reaches out to young people *who haven't acquired a functional command of the English language*.... My objections *have nothing to do with purism*...this book capitalizes on the *communicative handicaps of young African-Americans*, subtly suggesting they shouldn't be held to an expectation of *normal English* comprehension.... Rather than *accommodating the marginal literacy* of young black Americans, shouldn't we teach them how to communicate in *proper* and effective standard English?... [This book] targets Americans *who have failed to grasp English fundamentals*." (All italics are mine.)

I have some questions regarding this columnist's understanding of what's going on here. First, why does he assume that the young Black people at whom this book is directed "haven't acquired a functional command of the English language," have "communicative handicaps" and "marginal literacy," "have failed to grasp English fundamentals," and lack "normal English comprehension"? Why does he jump to these conclusions? I see nothing here to warrant these characterizations.

Andrew Young, former mayor of Atlanta and former United States ambassador to the United Nations, is quoted in the article as saying that *Black Bible Chronicles* will "reach many of our young people for whom the traditional language of faith has lost the power to bring them in touch with their God." There's nothing here that says that young Black people can't read or write "standard" English or comprehend the "traditional language of faith."

The columnist I quoted can't or won't accept the possibility that young Black people might prefer their language of worship to be their own particular hybrid Black English language, rather than the "proper and effective standard English" of the dominant white community—what the columnist calls "normal English." Is it really so hard to accept that, for many young Blacks, the "standard" White English of the *Bible* has, as Andrew Young says, "lost the power to bring them in touch with their God"?

Second, what if it were true (though I don't think it is) that the real reason *Black Bible Chronicles* was written for Black youth, and is attracting their attention, is because they "haven't acquired a functional command of" "standard" written English? Why is it so important to the columnist that young Black people do acquire this "functional command"? It's because his objections have everything (rather than "nothing") "to do with purism." He is disturbed by the fact that young Blacks, for whatever reason—whether it is by choice and preference, and/or due to "marginal literacy"—have rejected written White English in favor of written Black English. They've crossed the line in the sand!

The real problem here, in the eyes of the guardians of "standard" written English, is that a book like *Black Bible Chronicles* challenges the very dominance of European-Americans in the United States. The guardians correctly understand that the "standard" written languages of the Continental-European and European-American nations and communities are their last bastions of cultural purity, the purest (remaining) expressions of their cultures and values. Each of these nations has its official and unofficial language institutes, whose job it is to preserve its "standard" written language from alteration, adulteration, and hybridization.

These nations and their language institutes share the same rationale for preserving the purity of their written languages. It goes like this. We are the dominant cultures; the purist expression of our cultures is our "standard" written languages; the form of our languages is its content—which is that oppressed communities who write in our "standard" languages manifest and confirm, by that very act, that we are, in fact, dominant over them; when oppressed communities alter and hybridize the form of our "standard" written languages, it's an attack upon, an attempt to subvert, our dominance; therefore, oppressed communities won't be allowed to hybridize our "standard" written languages.

Sure, every year these institutes may allow a few more words and expressions from the oppressed communities' hybrid languages to appear in the "standard" lexicons. Major dictionary publishers seem to vie with each other to see who'll be the first to find and publish this year's new gems (safely labeling them "slang," "dialect," "vernacular," or "colloquial"). But rest assured, these institutes' literacy "police" won't permit these newcomer words to threaten the overall purity of the "standards."

Ironically, for all their complaints (like the columnist Steinback's against *Black Bible Chronicles*) that the oppressed communities misuse and/or aren't able to acquire a command of "standard" written English, many of these guardians (I'm not including Steinback here) *do not want* all, or even most, members of oppressed communities to become literate in "standard" written English.

I'll explain what I mean by returning to the second half of our original question, the part that asked why the slaveholders discouraged and forbade enslaved Africans from learning to read and write English.

Literacy has always been a political and economic issue. Historically, the elite and powerful classes within the oppressor nations and communities have reserved writing and reading for themselves, and it's still that way around the world. Lots of the Haves can read and write; lots of the Have-Nots can't. To the literate go the spoils, and to those with the spoils goes literacy.

In particular, oppressor communities haven't allowed the people of oppressed communities to learn to write and read because to do so *would allow the oppressed communities access to information and communication capabilities that could assist them in overthrowing their oppressors.*

In today's world, the literacy rates in oppressed, electronically-undeveloped countries are appallingly low. In the electronically-developed countries, official literacy rates are higher than in the electronically-undeveloped countries, but these rates can be deceiving. In the U.S., for example, many people who would be officially rated as literate—because they finished eighth grade, or according to some other index—aren't really functional writers/readers.

Official literacy rates for some oppressed communities inside the U.S. are as low or lower than literacy rates for some electronically-undeveloped countries. Estimates vary, but many sources agree that at least 80% of the world's people—several billions of people—are entirely nonliterate or functionally nonliterate. Most of the people in most of the world's linguistic communities have never even been given the chance to participate in literacy.

If Africans enslaved in the U.S. had been literate enough to read the newspapers, magazines, and books of the day, they could have learned much about their origins, about the nature and extent of the slave trade, possibly—through printed advertisements of slave auctions—about the whereabouts of family members, about Prosser's, Vesey's, Turner's and others' slave rebellions, about David Walker's *Appeal*, about the Abolitionist movement and Frederick Douglass' writings, about newspapers like the *Freedom Journal* out of Boston, about the underground railroad to Canada, about the *Creole's* and other slave ships' rebellions, about the runaway Maroon societies.

Literate captive Africans could also have studied the current problems and contradictions in the slaveholders' own society, and that study might have revealed to them chinks in what they might at first have perceived as an invulnerable, iron, white fist. The Africans could have then possibly exploited these divisions and weaknesses in white society in their centuries-long struggle to free themselves.

The pro-slavery white community knew that allowing the Africans literacy would have meant handing them the key to the databanks of the African and white communities—and that would have heralded the end of slavery.

As the institution of slavery matured in the U.S., however, new circumstances appeared which threatened the slaveholders' hegemony. Kidnapped Africans who could speak English—meaning, in most cases, one of the many Black Englishes—eventually constituted a population in the U.S. that far outnumbered the newly-arrived kidnapped Africans who couldn't. In one sense, the slaveholder had gotten what he'd wanted (as mentioned in "The Spoken-Language Question" section above): an African population that had mostly forgotten its native African languages and that could mostly speak only in English-related languages.

However, it began to dawn on the slaveholder that the situation wasn't all that rosy, because the Africans, no matter what their people, nation, or community of origin, were now able to communicate verbally with each other, via Black Englishes, on a grand scale—and that meant they could conspire on a grand scale.

Remember the "volatile contradiction" contained within the hybrid spoken languages of the oppressed that I referred to above? That contradiction was now beginning to turn in the Africans' favor. In the hybrid Black Englishes of the enslaved Africans, the aspect that at first had been primary (the "whiteness" of Black Englishes, expressing the Africans' subjugation to the slaveholders' language and values) now threatened to become secondary, and the aspect that had been secondary (the "Blackness" of Black Englishes, expressing the African communities' desire for self-determination) began to assert itself more and more.

Slowly the dynamic's compass needle was starting to edge away from bondage and point toward the stars of the "drinking gourd" in the Northern sky and the possibility of freedom. The desperate slaveholders tried to implement new tactics to strengthen their position against an increasingly incendiary African population, which far outnumbered the whites in many areas of the South. One of these tactics, I believe, was *to teach a handful of trusted Africans how to read and write.*

It must have been an amazing sight. Captive Africans of different origins, from different cultural and linguistic African communities, beginning to coalesce—right in the slaveholders' very backyards—into new communities united by new hybrid common cultures, spiritual beliefs, and spoken languages (Black Englishes).

The slaveholders' priority now, as it had always been, was to keep each African community divided and powerless. By bestowing literacy on a handful of trusted Africans, the slaveholders hoped to loosen (but not entirely destroy) those trusted individuals' ties to their captive communities, strengthen their bonds of loyalty to the slaveholders, and utilize them as agents (buffers, pacifiers, guards, punishers, and spies) in support of the slaveholders' interests against the interests of the masses of nonliterate Africans.

The slaveholder understood that written language, like spoken language, also has a historically key social function—but its function is the opposite of spoken language's. *Written languages divide us.* Specifically, a written language divides the members of a cultural community into literates and nonliterates—into those who can store and retrieve potentially vast amounts of information by writing and reading and those who can't.

The slaveholders' tactic, of dividing the African communities by creating a stratum of literate Africans, succeeded in some cases and backfired in others—a fact that was true then and is still true today. That's because this tactic forced upon the newly-literate African person a second "volatile contradiction": how were they going to use their new literacy skills, skills which potentially allowed them access to all of that previously-forbidden, stored information? Whereas the first "volatile contradiction" arose from the Africans' being able to speak the oppressor's language, this one arose from their being able to read and write it.

On the one hand, the newly-literate African could use the knowledge and information that they would store and retrieve to further their captive community's struggle to determine its own destiny: the road taken by such writers as David Walker, Frederick Douglass, and, more recently, James Baldwin, and Toni Morrison. On the other hand, they could put their literacy at the service of the very oppressor of their own community.

An example of the latter is the character Joe in African filmmaker Haile Gerima's extraordinary film, *Sankofa*. As an enslaved African child on a Southern plantation—probably the product of the slaveholder's rape of his mother—Joe was personally tutored in literacy and *Bible* studies by the slaveholder's own chaplain. He was then assigned to keep financial accounts and records and allowed to live the relatively more comfortable life of a "house" slave rather than that of a "field" slave.

When a pregnant African woman was captured after she had tried to escape from the plantation, she was strapped to a whipping pole and flogged relentlessly in front of the other Africans. As the one African who knew how to write numbers and count in English, Joe was commanded by the slaveholder to put his knowledge to "good" use by counting aloud the number of lashes the woman took across her back. Joe counted, lash after lash, until the woman died from the whipping.

Two powerful forces were pulling the newly-literate Africans in this perilous latter direction—in Joe's direction. First, any person from an oppressed community who becomes literate in the oppressor's "standard" written language, even if they strive to remain loyal to their community, is *distinct* from the great majority of that community's members. That is because they have the skills to do that which the oppressor can do, and which most members of their own oppressed community cannot do, and, in fact, are prevented from doing: to tap into the world's fund of information and knowledge using the oppressor's own written language. In this single respect, the literate oppressed individual stands *objectively* on the oppressor's side of the line—regardless of where they stand *subjectively*, regardless of where their heart and mind reside.

Second, by achieving literacy in "standard" White English, the individual has put themselves in danger of having their values shaped and molded by a medium that is, on the one hand, one of their oppressor's most effective values-transmitters and, on the other hand, as I said above, the very purest expression of those values.

Thus, when a captive African achieved literacy in the language of the slaveholder, they were doubly at risk. Not only did their learning to read and write the slaveholder's English set them apart from the majority of their community, but they had set out on a lifelong swim through the purest waters of Eurocentric culture and values. Would those currents pull them to the shores of Europe, or would they be able to resist the currents and navigate their way toward Africa? These were difficult choices that, following whatever collective discussion might have occurred between the literate African and their community, he or she ultimately had to resolve for themselves.

I'm identifying a social dialectic here, a dialectic that has been—and continues to be—an integral part of a greater process that could ultimately change the balance of power in the U.S. Short-term, the dominant European-American communities have had to teach a small number of oppressed People of Color to write and read in an attempt to use them to help maintain the status quo. Long-term, those oppressed people's becoming literate has been—and continues to be—part of the process that has prepared—and is preparing—some of them to carry and lead their communities' struggles for human rights to the next level.

What happens now if we introduce, into this volatile mix, new technology, which, by its very existence, will create the *potential opportunity* for everyone in the oppressed communities, whether literate or nonliterate, to access *all* stored information?

In a few years, talking computers will create the potential opportunity for everyone to deposit and withdraw all stored information orally-aurally and visually using graphics. In the VIVO Age that we're entering, each household VIVO, library VIVO, or wrist/lapel VIVO will become a great "spoken book," capable of textlessly transmitting, through speech and graphics, all of history's written documents and all of contemporary people's thoughts.

The question, then, as I say elsewhere in this book, becomes that of whether oppressed communities will be able to gain access to VIVO computers and turn this potential opportunity into actuality. For, if it could gain access to VIVOs, each oppressed community could orally program their own VIVOs in their own spoken native or hybrid language(s). If that were to happen, the withholding of literacy from oppressed communities by oppressor communities would no longer be a way that the latter could deny the former access to information.

Universal access to VIVOs would mean that nonliteracy would no longer keep oppressed communities from being able to access their own true histories. "Standard" written languages could no longer function as tools for burying the cultures and values of oppressed communities. Nor could they function as a wedge to weaken oppressed communities by dividing them into literates and nonliterates.

No people from oppressed communities would have to face that awful, second "volatile contradiction" of loyalty that formerly weighed (and still weighs today) upon the handful of literates from these communities—a contradiction they carried (and carry today) solely because they learned to read and write in the oppressors' languages.

In the VIVO Age, oppressed people will surely continue to have their hearts and minds tried and tested by other contradictions of loyalty to their communities, and they and their communities will have to struggle through these. But at least they won't have to struggle any longer with the contradictions caused by the oppressors' "standard" written languages.

I think it's no coincidence that the Civil Rights Movement of the 1960's in the United States gained momentum in the decade after television took hold in this country. The daily images and sounds beamed into living rooms via the 6 O' Clock News couldn't be ignored. The Black marchers, the Black leaders, the white mobs, the police dogs, the Black corpses, the racist politicians—these images and sounds united Black communities across the country and fueled the Movement's growth. Anger spilled over, consciousness got raised, communities got organized, demands got made, authority got confronted, victories got won. A small section of the white population who saw these images also began to demand justice and equality for Black people and an end to segregation.

By beaming all this into U.S. communities, and by allowing millions of people in the 1960's to access information that they would not have been able to access any other way, TV turned up the heat and had an impact. I believe that VIVOs will play a similar pivotal role in the global human rights struggles of the 21st Century—if the world's billions of people can gain access to VIVOs.

CHAPTER 10

Growing Oral Cultures in the VIVO Lab: Examining the Prospects for a Worldwide Oral Culture

Sometime early in the 21st Century, perhaps around 2010, all the nations and communities of the world, thanks to the invention of talking computers, will gain the *potential* capability to merge technologically, linguistically, and informationally. When that moment occurs, we will be standing at the threshold of a *worldwide* oral culture.

This doesn't mean that we will all be adopting the same culture or speaking the same language. It means that all nations and communities will potentially be able to use VIVOs (1) to access all stored information in the world, and (2) to speak to each other in their native languages using VIVO's simultaneous language-translator capability.

But this, the beginning of the 21st Century, is no time for naiveté. We've learned some hard lessons in our lifetimes. I prefer to speak about the new potentialities, rather than the new actualities or realities, of the VIVO Age because we need to constantly remind ourselves of two things.

First, until all of the world's nations and communities can actually acquire talking computers and begin to use them, they are relating to talking computers merely as a potentiality—merely as a technology that's been invented and that exists out there somewhere—but not as an actuality. We won't truly be a world-wide oral culture until people in every nation and community are wearing talking computers on their robes, in their pockets and lapels, or around their heads.

Second, the introduction of new technology, by itself, has never and will never change the world order. New technology may help us move toward a world community of nations and communities shaped by values such as self-determination, human rights, independence, equality, justice, cooperation, and peace, or it may help perpetuate the world we inhabit today, a world ruled by the opposite values. New technology can provide support for people's movements for social change, or it can be used by those with a stake in the status quo to try to crush those movements.

Only people's movements themselves, people united toward a common cause, and utilizing technology in the service of their cause, can change the world for the better.

The current worldwide political-economic system has proven amazingly resilient in being able to "commodify" new technology, defining uses and markets for the new technology that serve only to enrich those in power and strengthen their hold over most of the world's people. Left to its own devices (pun intended), this system will simply co-opt the new technology and sell it back to us in some form or other.

As it does now with cellular phones, AT&T will probably

give away free VIVOs—if we subscribe to their online service. Microsoft will probably do the same with their VIVO software— if we subscribe to their online service. And Macy's will probably give away the online service for free—if we use the service to buy X-dollars of Macy's merchandise each month. No free lunch—or new world order—here.

I ended Chapter 1 of this book by saying that, by 2050, the electronically-developed countries will be oral cultures and, by 2150, a worldwide oral culture will be in place.

What does that mean? What is an oral culture anyway? And how will being a worldwide oral culture change the look of societies and international human relations 150 years from now?

Yet more questions: what societal changes will we see as we walk these last several steps across the written-language bridge into the global—and extra-global, including outer space—orality of 2150? What clues are available today that can give us a glimpse of our future as oral culturians? What are the relevant questions we should be asking at this moment—the dawning of the Talking-Computer Age—with the first VIVOs soon to roll off the assembly lines?

Rather than attempting, in this final chapter of this book, to map the international, geopolitical mega-changes that VIVOs will produce, influence, or affect in the next century or two— an impossible task, anyway—I'm going to open up some questions and issues for further dialogue and study.

As far as I know, these issues are not being investigated today, nor are these questions even being asked. The worldwide oral culture of the 22nd Century has, until now, been an undiscovered land. By embarking on an intellectual and scientific journey to its shores, thinkers today can help shape the landscape that future generations will see when they arrive there.

One thing that being a worldwide oral culture means is that we will be going back to the future. We will be moving toward creating a worldwide information-storage-retrieval-communication system that in key ways mirrors or parallels the information-access systems found within linguistic societies of the ancient past.

What were their information-access systems like? They were oral-aural and non-text visual systems. Ours will be, too. They used human memory and picture-object methods of storing and retrieving information. Ours will rely on VIVO-computer memory and digital visuals.

In so-called "pre-literate" times, until the agricultural revolution took hold and spurred the creation of written languages, our ancestors had oral cultures, and they did just fine. They had science, the arts, religion, government, history, education, morality, medicine, law, entertainment, and every other kind of activity that we have today, although they didn't draw such sharp lines between these fields of endeavor as we do. They had everything that we'll have, and we'll have everything that they had. They didn't read and write—and neither will we.

Oral cultures aren't an extinct species. Although some nations and communities have been relying mainly on writing and reading to store and retrieve information for centuries, most nations and communities today are, and have always been, primarily oral cultures.

If it's true that oral cultures of the future will have certain parallels with oral cultures of the past and present, then examining oral cultures of the past and present could help us to find clues about the worldwide oral culture of the future. But how can we know which traits of past-present oral cultures will carry over into the future, and which won't? The temptation here is to think mechanically, to say things such as: since past oral cultures tended to be organized collectivistically or communally, future oral cultures will be, too.

This kind of mechanical thinking about the flow of history I call the "Hansel & Gretel" syndrome. It assumes, for example, that, for those of us living in electronically-developed societies, our own 21st Century trek from print to oral culturehood will actually move along the same steps—but in reverse order—that we took in our ancient trek from an oral to a print culture. It assumes that, by following VIVO's breadcrumb-strewn path into the future, we will necessarily be retracing our steps from our present social reality toward a future that will replicate our past social realities.

A momentary check on today's social reality, however, shows why we can't jump to any conclusions regarding which forms and shapes the world's nations and communities will take as they achieve universal orality by the 22nd Century. The following example shows why easy guesses just won't work.

While the electronically-developed countries are racing toward oral culture, a number of electronically-*un*developed countries are vigorously launching mass literacy campaigns. Eritrea, a country in the eastern "horn" of Africa that won its independence in 1991 after 30 years of fighting against colonialism, is one such country.

In the article "Eritrea, Dawn" (Duhl, F. and Gottesman, L., *Breakthrough*, Spring 1994, p. 8), two Eritrean women leaders are asked to describe their country's post-war priorities:

"'Women must be self-sufficient economically; politically they must be organized, as partners of men; and in their health situation, the community must be responsible to change the life of women because women are exposed to all the dangers of pregnancy and giving birth,' said Leteyesus [Negassi, head of the Project Department of Hamadaye, the National Union of Eritrean Women]. '*Along with literacy classes*** and advanced job training for women fighters, Hamadaye aims to provide small business loans—and these businesses, a roadside teashop or a tailorshop, are *small*—for the huge number of women who head households, a result of the war's devastation of Eritrea's families....'

"'Is there a backlash against women's gains,' we asked?

"'We expected it,' said Senait [Lijam, Hamadaye's educational coordinator]. 'We have, for example, opened an adult education center in Gash and Barka where most of the people are Muslims. The husbands say, "Hey, my woman should veil her face, and she's not going to go out of the house." We are not going to tell them to go against their religion. We don't care what religion they profess. *But it is a must that a woman should liberate herself from illiteracy.*** We insisted, and finally they accepted it.'" [**my emphasis]

In today's world, any analyst or commentator who takes a cavalier attitude toward literacy and the efforts of people seeking literacy is a fool. In developing countries like Eritrea, progressive leaders view their campaign to increase literacy as necessary for their nations' survival. They promote it as a key for improving their people's lives.

Without literacy, these leaders believe, quality education, quality healthcare, equality between women and men, participatory democratic government, a just legal system, employment opportunities and workers' rights, scientific and technological development, production of goods, trade and international relations, all civil and human rights, access to information and information technology, and a rising quality of life for all citizens wouldn't be possible. In Eritrea, the equality of women requires that women achieve literacy.

Now, what would it sound like if the author of *VIVO [Voice-In/Voice-Out]* were to say to the Eritrean people, "*Don't bother learning to read and write* because talking computers are going to make reading and writing obsolete in the near future"?

This is not something I could or would say. The Eritrean people, not I, will figure out what's best for them and what they need to do—in the short run and in the long run.

The world's nations and communities, due to their particular and unique histories, are entering the 21st Century with respectively different relationships to, and patterns of, literacy. Each society has a very different literacy-story to tell. Simple sets of statistics that claim to show the literacy rate of a nation's or community's population just can't capture the richness, the complexity, the truth of that story. That's because literacy-stories are qualitative, not quantitative.

"Uneven development" is the byword here. No two nations' or communities' histories are alike, so no two nations' or communities' literacy-stories are alike. Too many social forces are at work sculpting each story.

During a 1990 trip to Nicaragua, I had the privilege of briefly visiting the Garifuna community of Orinoco, located on the northern edge of Pearl Lagoon (Laguna de Perlas) on Nicaragua's eastern Atlantic-Caribbean coast, just north of the coastal city of Bluefields. The Garifunas—or Garinagu, a word meaning "people" which they also use to refer to themselves—are a "Black Carib" people who today live along the eastern coasts of several Central American countries, primarily Belize and Honduras. (The term "Carib" to refer to peoples of the Caribbean Basin has been disputed by some scholars, since it appears to be a word coined by colonial powers rather than a word any indigenous nation or people of the Caribbean used to describe or name themselves. For that reason, I'm placing it in quotation marks.)

The Garifunas are the descendants of a group of Africans who, in the late 1600's, escaped from a slave ship in the Caribbean and reached the Caribbean island of St. Vincent. On St. Vincent, the Africans intermingled with the indigenous "Island Caribs," themselves a mixture of the Arawak people, who originated thousands of years ago in the Orinoco-Amazon Basin of what is now Venezuela, and various other peoples, including the Tainos, indigenous to the Caribbean Basin.

For a hundred years, the "Black Caribs" of St. Vincent resisted French and British attempts to subjugate them until, in 1797, the British finally captured several thousand of them and forcibly relocated them to Roatan Island off the Atlantic-Caribbean coast of Honduras. From there, the "Black Caribs" migrated throughout the area, a small number of them settling in the Nicaraguan coastal community of Orinoco.

The language, which the "Island Caribs" of St. Vincent spoke before the Africans arrived, had its own extraordinary history. "The most salient characteristic, considered astounding by most observers, was that the men and women spoke different languages, the former of Carib origin, the latter Arawak.

"Supposedly, Carib conquerors, coming out of the Orinoco-Amazon Basin about a century before Columbus, had taken Arawak wives, who had perpetuated their own language among their children. In later years, as the boys spent more time with their fathers, they also became fluent in Carib, while the girls suffered along speaking only Arawak. While remnants of this male-female linguistic distinction survive, it is clearly Arawak that has won out, forming the basis of the language today known as Island Carib…." (from *Sojourners of the Caribbean*, p. 26, by Nancie L. Gonzalez, 1988, University of Illinois Press)

It was from the merger of "Island Carib" and African languages on St. Vincent, supplemented with elements of European colonial languages and Central American indigenous languages, that the unique Garifuna Creole language was born.

Fairly isolated from other Garifuna communities, the Garifunas of Orinoco, Nicaragua have almost entirely lost their Garifuna language. Now, only a handful of the community's populace, most of them elders, can still converse in Garifuna.

Until very recently, the Garifuna language was a spoken language only, although a few individuals, like Garifuna poet Marcella Lewis, have been transcribing their poems and prayers for years. We were told on our visit to Orinoco that a dictionary of the Garifuna language was in the process of being compiled by local linguists, and that Garifuna would soon become a complete written language as well. That dictionary—*The People's Garifuna Dictionary: Dimureia'gei Garifuna, Garifuna-Inglesi, English-Garifuna* (National Garifuna Council of Belize, 1993)—is now in print.

Thanks to the dictionary, it's now possible to store the complete Garifuna language via the written word—not just via the memories of the few elders who remember the language—and the potential for rescuing the language for use by future generations of Orinoco's Garifunas could greatly increase.

But it's not that simple. The fact that we have a written record of a language doesn't give life to that language. There are plenty of "dead" or "fossilized" written languages that no longer represent the living spoken languages of contemporary linguistic communities. Economic, political, and cultural forces beyond the Orinoco Garifunas' control are at work trying to wring the last drop of life out of their spoken Garifuna language and leave them (and us) with only its written "fossilized" remains between the covers of the linguists' dictionary.

In particular, two waves of non-Garifuna-speaking outsiders have cut deep inroads into the life of the Garifunas of Orinoco during the 19th and 20th Century, and have turned the Garifunas' spoken language into an endangered species.

First, in the 19th Century, came the English speakers who inhabited Nicaragua's Bluefields region: a mostly Black Creole people descended from English-speaking enslaved Africans who had escaped generations ago across the Caribbean from islands colonized by England and had intermixed with the indigenous Miskito people of Nicaragua's east coast and with Europeans.

By the mid-20th Century, as a result of generations of economic, political, religious, and social interaction between the smaller Garifuna community of Orinoco and the larger English-speaking Creole community of nearby Bluefields, Garifuna school children in Orinoco schools spoke, read, wrote, and were taught their lessons in English. The interaction I'm speaking about was very complex and had many other aspects to it. For instance, the influence exerted over Orinoco's Garifunas by their Bluefields Creole neighbors appears to have been more the result of the latter's political-economic-cultural dominance of this coastal region than the result of any conscious strategy on the Creoles' part to dominate the Garifunas or supplant their culture.

In addition, Moravian missionaries from the United States, Anglican missionaries, and missionaries of other denominations established churches in Orinoco which taught and encouraged the Garifunas to use the English language.

The second, and more recent, wave threatening the survival of the Garifunas' culture and language has been the influx of

Spanish-speaking Mestizos (descendants of the intermixing of Indigenous and European peoples) from the Pacific west coast of Nicaragua. Seeking improved economic opportunities, and, in some cases, dispersed by the Nicaraguan people's revolutionary war against the Somoza dictatorship in the 1970s and by the "Contra" battles in the 1980s, large numbers of Spanish-speaking Nicaraguans have migrated eastward to the Bluefields region in the last couple of decades.

These Spanish-speaking émigrés are rapidly succeeding in dominating the economy of the region. And, with economic domination, comes the power to dominate culturally. Not surprisingly, the schools of Orinoco are now teaching Garifuna school children their lessons in English and Spanish, with Spanish on the ascendancy. Young Garifunas, who have never learned to write or even speak the Garifuna language, are now speaking and becoming literate in two other languages. They've become a generation two giant steps removed from their linguistic roots.

We talked with Mira, her daughter Rina, and two young granddaughters on the porch of their simple woodframe house close to the busy Orinoco waterfront filled with small fishing boats and dugout canoes. Mira told us, in English, that she might be the last person in the community who remembered how to speak Garifuna, and that she had been trying to pass it on to the younger ones in the community before she died. But, she added, in her opinion, she wasn't really succeeding in her efforts. Her granddaughters, she said, spoke mostly Spanish and a little English.

Then Mira laughed and pointed at Rina and said that even her own daughter, Rina, couldn't speak Garifuna. When Rina heard Mira say that, Rina turned to us and said something in what must have been fluent Garifuna. Mother and daughter laughed, and so did we. Mira smirked and confessed that maybe she'd done a better job of teaching Garifuna to Rina than she'd thought.

We can see what an error it would be to try to portray this historically fertile, valiant, and somewhat tragic literacy-story-in-process with a simple statistic, such as "X percent of Orinoco's Garifuna population are nonliterate in year Y."

Let me pose some relevant questions for us to think about as the Eritreans, the Garifunas of Orinoco, and we in the electronically-developed countries charge into the 21st Century.

Q: Will the Garifunas, the Eritreans, and the other electronically-undeveloped countries and communities of the world be able to acquire VIVOs?

A: Today, there is a split in the power-elite class of the electronically-developed nations regarding whether their nations should share computer technology with electronically-undeveloped nations. One side says, "Sure, give them the hardware and software so we can sell them more software, access to the Internet, and all the products and services they wish to buy."

The other side says, "No way, we make hardware and software to make a profit—we're not just going to give it away. Plus, it would empower the electronically-undeveloped nations at our expense. Giving them the technology would allow them to duplicate and use it to compete economically, and perhaps wage war militarily, against the electronically-developed powers."

From the UNESCO/United Nations debates of the 1980s and 1990s, regarding whether the Have countries should share new technology with the Have-Not countries—not surprisingly, the Have-Nots lost—to the 1990s Clinton administration debates in the U.S. regarding sharing of encryption technology, these struggles among the power elites will continue into the VIVO Age.

Expect to see some or all of the following in our lifetime: (1) Legal bans against sending VIVOs and VIVO technology to Have-Not communities. (2) Keeping secret the methods of programming VIVOs. (3) Collecting and destroying "dangerous" data before it can be entered into VIVO memory banks. (4) Using coded or encrypted spoken languages to store and retrieve vital information in VIVOs. (5) Building and programming VIVOs so that they accept only the spoken languages of the Have nations and reject the spoken languages of the Have-Not nations. Might it only be a matter of time before we see the rise of a movement for an English-only Internet and for English-only VIVOs that reject instantaneous translation into other languages?

No one ever said that the price of freedom would be the sticker price of a new VIVO!

Q: If the electronically-undeveloped societies are able to acquire VIVOs, will they press on with their mass literacy campaigns, even as the world's electronically-developed nations and communities exchange their alphabets for oral cultures? Or will they jump directly from their traditional oral cultures to new VIVO-driven oral cultures, virtually skipping the print-literacy stage altogether?

A: Only the people of these societies themselves can and will answer this question. They shall continue to author their own literacy-stories—and their post-literacy stories.

Q: Will a VIVO-driven, worldwide oral culture strengthen local linguistic ties and reinforce local communities' use of their own native languages?

A: I believe it will. Because VIVOs will provide instantaneous translation among all spoken languages, there will be no technological rationales or reasons to replace local languages with dominant, outsider languages—though *technological* decisions will still be driven by *political* policies rooted in the reality of nations competing for domination or fighting for survival and liberation.

One-language-fits-all situations, such as English's role today as language-of-choice for conducting international business and commerce, and for worldwide communication on the Internet, will be eliminated, along with the time, effort, and expense it takes to teach a new language to nonspeakers of that language.

Furthermore, a community's traditional language is both a part of the community's culture and the glue that helps the community maintain its culture. If a community can keep its traditional language, it will also be easier for it to maintain its culture, its kinship ties, its sense of itself as a historical entity.

I'm not saying that, if any particular nation or community uses talking computers, it and its culture will surely survive. But using talking computers could work in favor of (though by no means guaranteeing) the survival of native languages and linguistic communities generally, in the face of the many social, cultural, political, and economic forces that will continue to work to tear these communities apart. Native languages will flourish in the VIVO Age.

Q: Will a worldwide oral culture serve to erase prejudicial and supremacist conceptions rooted in, and defined in terms of, print culture?

A: An interesting possibility to consider. Here's what I mean. Consider the present-day, pro-Eurocentric ideologies whose hold on our minds would be threatened by the end of writing and reading and by universal access to stored information through speech-driven technology. Many Western thinkers, for instance, divide the past into two primary periods: "history" and "prehistory." The period of "history," they say, began with written language, with the ability of humans to record in writing what was taking place in their lives. Everything before that must be considered "pre-history."

Hand-in-hand with that conceptual distinction goes the conceptual distinction between "civilization" and "pre-civilization," between "civilized" societies and "uncivilized" societies. "Civilized" societies, these same thinkers say, had/have, by definition—as a necessary condition of their being "civilized"—a written language. "Uncivilized" societies are those that lacked/lack a written language, and are sometimes euphemistically called "pre-literate" or, more disparagingly, "primitive."

These two distinctions are often used to support each other by certain thinkers who insist that "history" and "civilization" began in the West, in ancient Greece—or, with a stretch, maybe in ancient Egypt, which they have traditionally characterized as a unique "white" society on the African continent—or maybe somewhere else, as long as it wasn't in Black Africa, or Asia, or the Americas before Columbus.

In the first place, these two ideological distinctions, based as they are on having or not having a written language, will not be able to be applied in the same way, to the same countries, in the 21st Century. In 2050, if anyone will be reading and writing, it will be the Eritreans and the Garifunas, not tomorrow's citizens of today's electronically-developed countries.

In the text-less milieu of the electronically-developed nations, it will be absurd to point to written language as a *defining aspect* of "our superior" society, and to the lack of written language as a *defining aspect* of "their inferior" society. There simply won't be any written language to point to in "our" society. Perhaps intransigent Eurocentrists will decide to reverse the definitions, labeling "our" society "superior" because we will have replaced those outdated, alphabetic chicken-scratches with the glory of natural speech and talking computers.

Is it possible that, the longer we in the electronically-developed Western nations live with VIVOs, that is, the longer we live without using written language, the more culturally, intellectually, and emotionally *identified* we might become with those societies of the past/present that survived/survive and thrived/thrive without written language? Might we have less trouble—unlike certain Western thinkers today—affirming these oral cultures and including them within the ranks of "civilized" societies which existed/exist in a "historical" era?

Might we even arrive at a moment in history when these value-laden distinctions—which infuse an "It's the Best!" connotation into terms like "the West" and "Western Civilization"—will lose all credibility and disappear? A moment when we can say, "Bye, bye, 'West is Best.' Welcome, World?" That would be a true VIVOlution.

Finally, the questions crowding this chapter suggest a new way of looking at human history. Most—though not all—human societies began as oral cultures. Some of these societies have transformed or are transforming themselves into text-based cultures, using written language to freeze and thaw information, while other societies have remained oral cultures. In the 19th and 20th Centuries, some of the text-based societies, spurred by the invention of the phonograph, began to transform themselves again into oral cultures—a process that will continue to unfold throughout the 21st Century.

This evolutionary progression—from oral culture to print-based culture to oral culture or, alternatively, from oral culture directly to VIVO-aided oral culture—is one that we can chart for each and every society. We can represent each society's unique process as a curve on a graph, which will allow us to visualize not only its course from past to present, but also its future course based on our study of past and present data.

Overlaying all the graphs will allow us to see the full range of uneven development as the world's nations and communities continue to rework their literacy-stories, nonliteracy-stories, and post-literacy-stories to fit their 21st Century needs and desires (Figure 8).

[8]

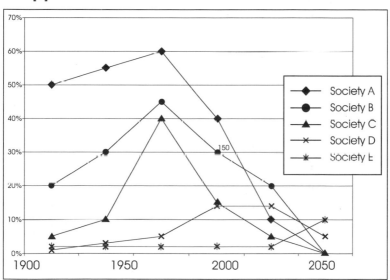

Percent of population 14 years old or older that is functionally literate.

As we compile this view of human history, however, let's do it cautiously, remembering that graphs, like percentages, are quantitative, and that no curves or graphs can portray the deep and intricate realities of Mira's, Rina's, Leteyesus's, Senait's, and our own languages and lives.

Epilogue

FAQ's with A's:
Frequently Asked Questions
with Answers

Q: You say that if a nonliterate person will be able to use a voice-in/voice-out (VIVO) computer to write perfectly, it shows that written language will be obsolete and on the way out. I don't understand. Doesn't it show that written language will be even more useful and important since, with VIVOs, everyone will be able to use written language to store and retrieve information?

A: No. It shows that written language will be a redundant technology, merely adding an unnecessary and superfluous step to all information accessing by requiring speech to be translated into text. Why should we do the job orally-aurally, and then do it again via writing and reading, when doing it just orally-aurally would get the job done?

Q: They said that TV would replace the radio—and they

were wrong! You're just as wrong when you say that voice recognition and VIVOs will replace reading and writing. Written language is central to our way of life; it's an incredible invention, and it's not going away. Just as TV and radio coexist now, written language and voice-recognition technology will continue to coexist far, far into the future. What's your reason for thinking they won't?

A: Written language is an incredible invention, but the fields of human history are littered with incredible inventions and technologies that were made obsolete by newer inventions and technologies. And, while written language has played a central role for a minority of people in a minority of societies around the world, it has never become central to the lives of most people. That's the problem! Those who said TV would replace radio didn't understand that, although TV and radio do the same general job—convey information—radio has an advantage over TV. Radio doesn't require that we focus our eyes on a screen; we can drive a car or make a salad while listening. Although text and VIVOs also do the same general job—store and retrieve information—text has no advantage that will withstand the onslaught of the four "engines" driving us into the VIVO Age.

Q: What are those four "engines"?

A: (1) Evolutionarily/genetically, humans are driven to speak. (2) Technologically, humans are driven to develop technologies that allow us to access information by speaking. In addition, we tend to replace older technologies, like text, with newer ones that will do the same job more quickly, efficiently, and universally. (3) Young people in the electronically-developed countries are, en masse, rejecting text as their technology of choice for accessing information in favor of speech-driven and non-text, visual-driven technologies. (4) The billions of functionally nonliterate people worldwide want access to information, computers, and the Internet without first having to become literate.

Q: Why do you think the computer industry will take the trouble to research, develop, and produce VIVOs when text-driven computer systems are working just fine?

A: A huge demand, ready markets, and huge profits. VIVOs, being nonliterate-user-friendly, fit the needs of governments, corporations, businesses, and agencies in countries around the world. The workforces in the great majority of countries—including the electronically-developed countries—are mostly nonliterate or semi-literate. Employers will soon realize that, once they install VIVOs in their facilities, they will be able to open up their information-handler labor pools to nonliterate employees. Also, nonliterate individuals will want VIVOs for all the same reasons that literate individuals want text-driven computers today. In addition, the computer industry, like everyone else in the electronically-developed countries, is responding (albeit mostly unconsciously) to the human evolutionary drive to return to our biogenetic, pre-alphabetic, spoken-language roots.

Q: If VIVOs are going to replace written language, and no one is going to read or write anymore, won't that result in a massive "dumbing down" of society? Don't we need to be able to read and write in order to really think—especially to think logically and scientifically?

A: No. The end of reading and writing doesn't mean the end of thought, thinking, or language. Written language is a technology humans invented to help store and retrieve information under a particular set of rapidly changing social and environmental conditions 6,000 to 10,000 years ago known as the agricultural revolution. The nonliterate peoples who created written language already thought logically and scientifically—

which is why they were able to create written language in the first place. As is true with most technologies, written language will be replaced by another technology—in this case, VIVOs— which will do the same job of storing and retrieving information more easily, quickly, efficiently, cheaply, and universally.

Q: Using written language/text is an extremely efficient way to scan and search for information. Won't scanning and searching for information orally-aurally, using VIVOs, be much less efficient?

A: No, using VIVOs will be more efficient. First, we have to drop our text-based models when we think about searching for information with VIVOs. Using text, we can rapidly scan lists, indexes, paragraphs, and pages of data; when we try to imagine listening to all these words, it seems a much harder and slower process. But we won't listen to all the words. We'll search by conversing with the VIVO—just as we usually converse with each other. If I want to find out what hippopotamuses eat, I don't usually ask you to tell me everything about hippos and wait and listen for data about their feeding habits. I just ask you, "What do hippos eat?" and you tell me.

Q: Won't using VIVOs rather than reading and writing text make us less visual?

A: No, it will make us more visual. It will also make us more aural, tactile, olfactory, and gustatory. We print-literates are not very visual compared to people who live in oral cultures. Our eyes have been trained to recognize text but not much else. This singling out of one sense organ, our eyes, and focusing it on a static reality, text, in order to process information happens only among print-literates. People in oral cultures process information by continuously focusing all five senses interactively on a dynamic, changing reality. This interactive unity of our

senses working to understand the world is at the root, historically and etymologically, of our idea of "common sense." As we
lose written language and move toward oral culture, we'll
heighten both our visuality and our common sense.

Q: It requires huge amounts of storage space in a computer's
memory to store sound/speech—much more than it takes to
store the same information in the form of text. And since this
much memory costs big bucks, who is going to buy these very
expensive talking computers?

A: Everybody—except that VIVOs won't be that expensive. The industry will invent ways to compress storage space,
making storage more efficient and requiring less memory.
Memory itself will become cheaper. Take, for example, the way
the industry has dealt with the high cost of storing computer
graphics. To paraphrase Nicholas Negroponte in *Being Digital*:
The more pixels, the more memory you need. A typical screen
with 1000 x 1000 pixels in full color needs 24 million bits of
memory. In 1961, memory cost $1. per bit. By 1995, 24 mil-
lion bits of memory cost $60.

Q: Won't the fact that no one else will be able to read or
write make it easier for the power elite to exploit them in the
21st Century? Won't the power elite use written language as a
way to keep information secret and inaccessible from the
nonliterate masses—that is, from all of us?

A: The situation you describe has been happening ever since
the invention of written language and explains why billions of
the world's people have been kept nonliterate. Actually, the power
elite won't use written language to keep information secret in
the future because manipulating computer-driven written lan-
guage/text will be too inefficient compared with manipulating
VIVO-driven spoken language. They'll use secret spoken, coded-

sound and/or coded-non-text-visual VIVO languages.

Q: You talk about the potential opportunities VIVOs hold for the billions of nonliterate and semi-literate people of the world. But won't these people have just as hard a time acquiring VIVOs in the 21st Century as they had acquiring text-driven computers in the 20th?

A: Yes. I believe that access to the world's storehouse of information and knowledge is a human right. The struggle to acquire the VIVO technology that will turn these potential opportunities into actuality will be a major human rights contest of the 21st Century.

Q: Won't we lose that wonderful attachment to reading and writing that so many of us love? Won't we lose great written literature, great creative writing?

A: Yes. That deep attachment that some people have to reading and writing will, in most cases, be supplanted by a new appreciation of, and attachment to, listening and speaking—the type of love affair with speech that existed/exists in oral cultures of the past and present. Of course, there will be some individuals who will continue to read and write as a hobby simply because they enjoy it, just as there are some individuals who continue to make their own furniture and churn their own butter even though they don't have to. And great literature and creative writing? They'll be replaced by great storytelling, great spoken poetry, and great creative speaking. Remember that creative written language is the child of creative spoken language and that both involve creative thinking and the creative use of language.

Q: In the future, we'll be using lots of universal visual symbols and icons to convey information. Won't we have to know how to read and write them? Won't they actually be a kind of written language?

A: We will definitely continue to use visual symbols and icons as a way to store and retrieve information and will definitely have to know how to draw and interpret them. But we won't be reading and writing these symbols and icons, and they won't constitute a written language—even if they're strung or linked together.

Reading and writing are activities that apply only to a written language; however, visual symbols and icons are not written language. A written language needs rules of syntax and semantics that tell how to string its symbols together and how to interpret the meaning of such strings. There is no single set of rules that tells how to combine and interpret universal symbols and icons. The first pictographs of Chinese language may have begun as solitary "universal" symbols, but they became a language only after they were linked according to syntactic and semantic rules. Our ancestors' cave and rock drawings contained many visual symbols and icons, but we don't consider their drawings to be a written language. Say I lined up three universal symbols—"woman," "man," and "smile"—in some order and asked you to tell me the meaning of this sequence. Without being given any rules to follow, you would have no way of knowing who, if anyone, was smiling, or at whom.

Q: You say that written numerals will also disappear. Then how will mathematicians, physicists, and other scientists do theoretical mathematics? Won't they still have to use numerals in the future?

A: I'm not a mathematician, and, to be honest, I don't know how theoretical math will be done in the future, but I'm sure that it won't rely on the written numeral system we use today. Numerals are too complicated and inefficient a way to store, retrieve, and communicate mathematical information. Combinatorics, a specialty area of geometry, already employs non-numeral visual-language systems, so this is not a far-fetched idea. I imagine that theoretical math will be entering new conceptual realms in the 21st Century that even today's mathematicians cannot conceive. And the ways that future mathematicians will decide to visually represent these realms are likewise unknowable today.

Q: Just because you've been able to come up with a theory about something that could possibly happen in the future doesn't mean it's necessarily going to happen, right?

A: Right. But today's clues and road signs do all seem to be pointing in the same direction: toward an oral culture in the electronically-developed countries by 2050.

About the Author

Villiam Crossman is a philosopher, futurist, and professor involved with issues of education, media and technology, language and culture, and human rights. He is Founder/Director of the CompSpeak 2050 Institute for the Study of Talking Computers and Oral Cultures www.compspeak2050.org. He has spoken at conferences and meetings around the world, appeared frequently on TV, radio, and online, and served as a consultant for governmental and non-governmental agencies, think tanks, educational institutions, research and development centers, and corporations. In a special millennium issue (Dec. 2, 1999), the *New York Daily News* cited William Crossman as one of six key visionaries for the 21st Century, along with physicist Stephen Hawking, astronaut Jim Lovell, Internet pioneer Vint Cerf, scientist Ray Kurzweil, and bioethicist Art Caplan. A list of recent articles by and about the author appears on his website.

Crossman has presented his controversial, thought-provoking views about talking computers and other future-related issues to such diverse groups as the U.S. Government Institute of Museum and Library Services, International Convocation of Academies of Engineering & Technology Sciences—CAETS, NASA's Goddard Space Flight Center, Adelaide International Artists' Festival 2000 (Australia), U.S. National Parks Chiefs of Interpretation and Education Conference, Technical Association of the Pulp and Paper Industry—TAPPI International Conference, Maryland Public Libraries Technology Conference, Technology in Education International Conference—TechED, World Future Society, E-vision Digital Media Center (New Zealand), Lernout and Houspie Voice Recognition, Finland Futures Research Centre, University of California-Santa Cruz' Perceptual Science Lab, The Vision Center for Futures Creation (Sweden), Georgia Tech University's Digital Signal Processing Lab, Italian Public TV Network, and Radio New Zealand.

The author received his B.A. in philosophy from Cornell University, his M.A. in philosophy from Harvard University, and continued his study of philosophy and linguistics at The Massachusetts Institute of Technology.

During a lengthy teaching career, Crossman has taught an eclectic mix of university and college courses in his areas of academic expertise, which include philosophy, critical thinking, writing, and English as a second language. While a graduate student at Harvard, he taught writing to Harvard freshmen. After studying at M.I.T., he joined the philosophy faculty at Tufts University. Since then, he has taught at a variety of academic institutions including City College of San Francisco, San Francisco State University, and Antioch College West. For eight years (1989-1997), Crossman taught at Morris Brown College, a historically-Black college in Atlanta, Georgia. He is currently teaching at Vista Community College in Berkeley, California.

The author is a longtime organizer/activist in the anti-racism and pro-human rights movements, a jazz pianist, and a poet. He lives in Oakland, California and can be contacted through his website.

Bibliography—Works Cited

Affleck, Ben and Damon, Matt, screenwriters, *Good Will Hunting*, film; Miramax Films, 1997. [p. 137]

Baldwin, James, "If Black English Isn't a Language, Then Tell Me, What Is?" from *Revelations: An Anthology of Expository Essays By and About Blacks*, Redd, Teresa M., editor; 1993, Ginn Press; p. 281. [pp. 155-156]

Burton, Robert, *Anatomy of Melancholy*, 1621; cited in *O.E.D.*, p. 573. [p. 107]

Davis, Erik, "Game Over," *Wired Magazine*, Vol. 8, No. 2, February, 2000. [pp. 46-47]

Davis, Ossie, "The English Language Is My Enemy," from *Revelations: An Anthology of Expository Essays By and About Blacks*, Redd, Teresa M., editor; 1993, Ginn Press; pp. 3-4. [pp. 154-155]

Diller-Quaile, *1st Solo Book for Piano*; ca. 1915, Schirmer Publishers, New York. [pp. 139, 145]

Duhl, Frank and Gottesman, Les, "Eritrea Dawn," in *Breakthrough Journal*, Vol. 18, No. 1, Spring, 1994, San Francisco; p. 8. [pp. 175-176]

Dylan, Bob, "Subterranean Homesick Blues," from *Bringing It All Back Home*, released March 22, 1965, Columbia Records. [p. 11]

Genesis, Book of, Old Testament, *Bible*. [pp. 86, 160-161]

Gerima, Haile, director/screenwriter/producer, *Sankofa*, film; Mypheduh Films, Inc. Studio, 1993 [p. 167]

Gingerich, P.D. et al, "Origin of whales from early artio-dactyls." *Science* 293, Sept. 21, 2001; pp. 2239-2242. Artist: J. Klausmeyer/*Science*. [p. 76]

Gonzalez, Nancie L., *Sojourners of the Caribbean*, 1988; University of Illinois Press; p. 26. [pp. 178-179]

Hamilton, Sir William, *Reid's Works*, 1842; cited in *O.E.D.*, p. 573. [p. 107]

McCary, P. K., *Black Bible Chronicles: From Genesis To The Promised Land/Book One*; 1993; African American Family Press. [pp. 160-162]

"NASA develops system to computerize silent, 'subvocal speech,'" *NASA News*, Ames Research Center, National Aeronautics and Space Administration, Moffett Field, California; March 17, 2004; Release: 04-18AR. [pp. 123-124]

Negroponte, Nicholas, *Being Digital*, 1995; Alfred A. Knopf, New York. [pp. 118-119, 193]

Oxford English Dictionary (O.E.D.), Second Edition, Vol. III; Clarendon Press, Oxford; p. 573. [p. 107]

People's Garifuna Dictionary, The: Dimureia'gei Garifuna, Garifuna-Inglesi, English-Garifuna; 1993; National Garifuna Council of Belize. [p. 179]

Searchinger, Gene, *Discovering The Human Language*, 1995; Nova Video Series, Public Broadcasting System TV. [p. 98]

"Spelling Skills Decline in Germany," *The Week in Germany*, April 17, 1998; German Information Center, New York, NY; reprinted in *The Futurist*, November, 1998, World Future Society, Bethesda, MD. [pp. 104-105]

Steinback, Robert L., "Don't Rap the Bible," *The Atlanta Journal/The Atlanta Constitution*, October 5, 1993, Op-Ed Page article. [pp. 160-163]

Index